ltural Theory and the Problem of Modernity

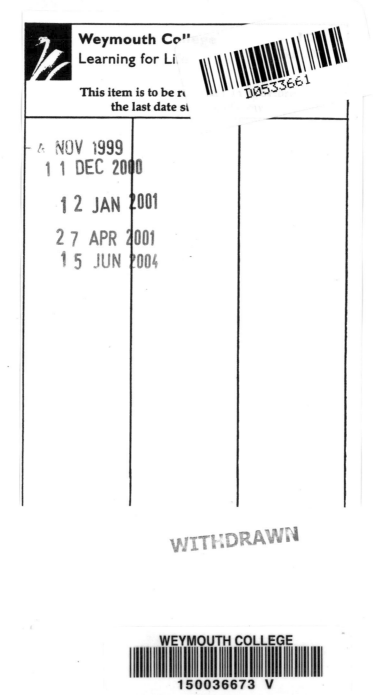

Weymouth Co''
Learning for Li

This item is to be r
the last date s

D0533661

4 NOV 1999
1 1 DEC 2000
1 2 JAN 2001
2 7 APR 2001
1 5 JUN 2004

WITHDRAWN

Also by Alan Swingewood

A Short History of Sociological Thought (2nd edn)
Sociological Poetics and Aesthetic Theory
The Myth of Mass Culture

Cultural Theory and the Problem of Modernity

Alan Swingewood

First published 1998 by
MACMILLAN PRESS LTD
Houndmills, Basingstoke, Hampshire RG21 6XS
and London
Companies and representatives
throughout the world

ISBN 0–333–61341–4 hardcover
ISBN 0–333–61342–2 paperback

A catalogue record for this book is available from the British Library.

This book is printed on paper suitable for recycling and made from fully managed and sustained forest sources.

10   9   8   7   6   5   4   3   2   1
07   06   05   04   03   02   01   00   99   98

Printed in Hong Kong

Published in the United States of America 1998 by
ST. MARTIN'S PRESS INC.,
Scholarly and Reference Division,
175 Fifth Avenue, New York, N.Y. 10010

ISBN 0–312–21508–8 cloth
ISBN 0–312–21509–6 paperback

Contents

Introduction

The 1980s and 1990s have witnessed an explosion of interest in the study of culture. If alienation, ideology and hegemony had been the key words of earlier periods, culture was now the dominant concern for the humanities and social sciences. Although it had always occupied an important place within the various humanist disciplines, culture had tended to become assimilated to literary and aesthetic analysis (culture forming a background and context) or to the study of social structure, social institutions and social change (culture as socialisation). As for Marxism, one of the major intellectual currents of the post-war years, culture came to enjoy a shadowy presence and problematic status frequently identified as a form of ideology and analysed as a reflection of specific class and political interests yet signifying a critical realm of human values and aspirations. What was common to Marxist, literary and social studies, however, was a failure to adequately *theorise* culture and develop specific concepts for the analysis of its internal properties, the variety of its forms and links with human activity and the complex, highly differentiated structures of modern society. The rise of cultural studies during the 1960s (in the widely different work of Richard Hoggart, E. P. Thompson and Stuart Hall, with its institutional setting the Centre for Contemporary Cultural Studies at the University of Birmingham) had emphasised the social aspects of culture (it was not simply about art and literature but concerned with communication and community) without generating a necessary sociological framework and conceptual tools. The breakup of cultural studies into specialist areas of media, feminism and ethnicity, a process influenced by new, largely European theories of politics, ideology, discourse and the subject, further shifted the study of culture away from sociology.

However, one result of these developments was to broaden the definition of culture away from its narrow identification with literature and art to include fashion and food, sport and advertising, journalism and everyday life, as well as working-class subcultures characterised by various forms of ritual and resistence to the dominant social values. As E. P. Thompson has pointed out, culture is

> a clumpish term which by gathering up so many activities and attributes into one common bundle may actually confuse or disguise discrimina-tions...We need to take this bundle apart and examine the components with more care: rites, symbolic modes, the cultural attributes of hegemony, the inter-generational transmission of custom and custom's evolution within historically specific forms of working and social relations. (Thompson, 1993, p.13)

In this book I attempt to unravel the various meanings of culture and develop a distinctive sociological approach, to theorise culture sociologically. For while culture has become critical for contemporary studies, its meaning has been influenced by a bewildering range of theoretical frameworks and theorists (such as those of Althusser, Foucault and Baudrillard) in which linguistic and discourse analysis together with postmodernism advance concepts and methods alien to the sociological study of culture. Historically the study of culture as a separate and distinct realm, with its own specific internal properties, was closely linked to philosophy and anthropology. At the end of the eighteenth century culture was largely identified with the idea of civilisation, with holisitic concepts such as a world view or 'mentality'. Williams notes its original meaning as 'to cultivate', the tending of natural growth as in agriculture, but by 1800 the word signalled the transition from nascent industrialism to capitalism and modernity. In the course of the nineteenth century culture increasingly became intellectualised, identified with habits of mind and humane values, defined idealistically in terms of the arts and 'high' rather than 'low' or 'ordinary' culture. In England culture constituted an aesthetic and literary discourse centred on the perfection of humanity, the creation of universal values, 'sweetness and light' in opposition to a dehuman-ising and ugly machine civilisation. In the works of Matthew Arnold

(1822–88) culture is defined as a body of creative work (literary texts) which embodies high moral values, a rejection of industrialism, materialism and philistinism. Culture is social in so far as it affirms a civilising mission, although narrowly conceived in terms of texts which generate binary divisions such as high versus low. This culture and society tradition becomes further developed in the work of F. R. Leavis, T. S. Eliot and Raymond Williams, the first-named forging a contrast between pre-industrial culture (which hecalled 'organic' and community-based) with twentieth-century industrial, capitalist mass culture built around atomistic social relations. In an important sense the literary critic Leavis and the poet and critic Eliot were largely responsible for socially contextualising culture and initiating the debate on mass culture, popular culture and minority culture in English literary studies. I examine this approach in Chapter 5, arguing that this idealist notion of culture, while bound up with high art forms, is nevertheless based in the idea of community and social experience. Culture is a whole way of life embracing texts and community values, in Eliot's words, 'the characteristic activities and interests of a people'. Culture was normative, critical of industrialism, affirming tradition, universal values and a sense of historical continuity.

In a similiar vein, Williams defines culture holistically as a whole way of life, as ordinary and more closely linked with everyday life than in the Leavis–Eliot model. In effect, Williams seeks to unify the literary approach to culture with the anthropological. It was E. B. Tylor who argued that all societies, of every type and at all stages of social development possess a culture. Culture is not coterminous with civilisation but constitutes 'that complex whole which includes knowledge, belief, art, morals, law custom and other capabilities acquired by man as a member of society' (Tylor, 1958, p. 1). Through values and symbols, individuals are able to communicate and form communities within the whole. Early anthropological approaches to culture tended to adopt a functionalist standpoint, values and symbols working to promote social cohesion. But one of the main problems with such holistic notions is their relevance to modern complex, highly differentiated societies, with their multiple social groups and classes. In modern society there exist many different ways of life bound up with issues of ideology and power, with complex patterns of social conflict and social struggles. There is, too, the question of meaning and action: Tylor's definition of culture conceives it in material not idealistic terms without raising the problem of its *making*.

Contemporary anthropological approaches to studying culture have sought to modify this excess of materialism by arguing that culture involves 'an historically transmitted pattern of meanings embodied in symbols, a system of inherited conceptions expressed in symbolic forms by means of which men communicate, perpetuate, and develop their knowledge about and attitude toward life' (Geertz, 1973, p. 89). Clifford Geertz's more subtle concept of culture has been widely influential, especially in those sociological approaches to cultural analysis which focus on beliefs, values and symbols as the constituent elements of culture.

Distinguishing anthropological from sociological concepts of culture is difficult if a purely internal approach is adopted. In this book I am concerned both with the sociology of culture and the relation of culture to modernity. As I argue in Chapter 8, sociology is closely related to the project of modernity, to the development of highly differentiated societies which provide the institutional basis for the autonomy of culture and a reflexive individual. Culture, in other words, is about norms, values and symbols but, as Geertz noted, it is equally about meaning and action. A sociological perspective is one which locates culture in terms of its social basis, in modernity, and the complex meanings it both embodies and generates through social action.

But I think it needs emphasising that the boundaries between sociological and anthropological concepts of culture are fluid and frequently overlap. Durkheim, for example, in his study of early religion in pre-modern societies (notably the Australian aborigines) analyses culture sociologically, as a signifying system that produces collective representations (totems for example) through which individuals develop a sense of identity with the whole society. Collective representations are one of the means whereby society achieves integration, but the point is that Durkheim's approach to culture emphasises the meanings which symbols have for individual members. Equally, Weber defined culture as the realm of meaning which constituted the basis of social action and social change. In Chapters 2 and 4, Weber's and Durkheim's theories of culture are examined, Weber advancing the important concept of the 'relative autonomy' of culture, culture as values, symbols and practices which, in the period of modernity, possess their own distinctive logic and structure. Durkheim, too, with his notion of culture as collective representations, seeks to establish a partly autonomous cultural realm. It is this aspect of culture which is further developed in interactionist sociology, especially in Goffman's work on the interaction order in which specific symbolic forms based on ritual and shared meaning enable individuals to produce a complex notion of self.

In contrast, functionalist approaches to culture analyse symbolic forms (ritual, myth and codes) for the ways they maintain social order and integration, assimilating meaning to the process of socialisation and effectively marginalising the active role of human agents in the production of culture. As I argue in Chapter 1, some versions of Marxism adopt this functionalist perspective, theorising culture as ideology, as a reflex of external material conditions and an expression of class interests: culture as social cement binding individuals collectively to the core values of capitalism. However, this reductive notion has been challenged by culturalist Marxists as Gramsci, Adorno and Bakhtin. Chapters 1 and 3 address the problem of culture conceived in its integral relation with social struggles and power relations, practices and meaning. Culture is less a way of life than sites of struggle imbricated in ideology and politics, overlaid with issues of gender, race and generation. Culture is not the expression or the representation of class, but the active articulation of complex identity.

Culture, then, is the realm of meaning, of values and symbols, located in specific structural contexts. The problem of contextualism is one of the most critical issues of cultural theory, that as culture is produced within contexts it must never be reduced to context. In Chapter 6 I examine one recent sociological theory of context, Bourdieu's concept of field, and the attempt to integrate the principle of partial autonomy of culture with capitalist industrialisation and social change. Bourdieu's concept of culture, like that of Gramsci, links it with social struggle and an open rather than closed notion of society. For while culture is concerned with meaning it is not a fixed and completed meaning, since while bound to context, culture goes beyond it by affirming the irreducible pluralism of social life. One of the major themes of the sociology of culture, from Parsons to Gramsci, the Frankfurt School, Weber and Durkheim to Bourdieu and Bakhtin, is that culture generates universal elements that in some way transcend historical contexts. Chapter 7 explores Bakhtin's historical sociology of culture and its attempt to develop a concept of culture which is the product not simply of social struggle but of dialogue between different voices and standpoints: Bakhtin's dialogic principle is one that suggests culture as the realm of open, unfinished and multiple meanings.

Raymond Williams has noted that cultural sociology was a 'late entry' into sociology 'after the hard stuff of class, industry and politics', with its development 'little more than a loose grouping of specialist studies either of communications...the media or...the arts' (Williams, 1981, p. 9). A new kind of sociology is now required to deal with culture: this book is an attempt to engage with this problem.

Chapter 1

Theorising Culture: Marxism

Towards the end of his life, irritated by what he considered to be profound misinterpretations of his work, especially by self-proclaimed Marxists, Marx vigorously protested: 'All I know is that I am not a Marxist' (Marx and Engels, 1962, vol. 2, p. 486). And in a similarly iconoclastic spirit, Engels attacked the facile assumption that Marxism was no more than a sophisticated theory of economic and historical determinism:

> according to the materialist conception of history the ultimately determining element in history is the production of real life. More than this neither Marx nor I have ever asserted. Hence, if somebody twists this into saying that the economic element is the *only* determining one, he transforms that proposition into a meaningless, abstract, senseless phrase. The economic situation is the basis, but the various elements of the superstructure : political forms of the class struggle and its results...constitutions... juridicial forms...philosophical theories, religious views...exercise their influence upon the course of the historical struggles and, in many cases, preponderate in determining their form. (ibid., p. 48).

It is this reciprocal interaction between the economic 'base' and the cultural or ideological 'superstructure' which necessarily results in the specific 'historical event'. But as Engels continued, 'Marx and I are ourselves partly to blame for the fact that the younger people sometimes lay more stress on the economic side than is due to it.' The broad tendency of social theory before Marx had been to minimise the role played by economic forces in historical and cultural development in favour of 'ideal' elements, notably political religious and philosophical

1

ideas. It was as a reaction to this non-materialist perspective that Marx and Engels were led to overstate the constituting role of economic forces and, in their theoretical formulations, to subordinate culture as the realm of the 'ideal', to economic necessity. But, as Engels pointed out, when their analysis moved from the abstractly theoretical and methodological to close, empirical studies of distinct historical periods due weight was always accorded to the 'ideal' elements at work. For in analysing specific historical contexts (especially in Marx's *The Class Struggles in France*, 1850, and *The Eighteenth Brumaire of Louis Bonaparte*, 1852) emphasis was given to the active role played by ideas and culture within the economic and political structure. Analysing the revolutionary crises that gripped France in 1848, Marx noted the complex balance of forces at work within both the economic and political structures and the differentiation and plurality of social classes, going on to suggest, in one of his most brilliant passages that

> Men make their own history, but they do not make it just as they please; they do not make it under circumstances chosen by themselves, but under circumstances directly encountered, given and transmitted from the past. The tradition of all the dead generations weighs like a nightmare on the brain of the living. And just when they seemed engaged in revolutionising themselves and things, in creating something that has never yet existed, precisely in such periods of revolutionary crisis, they anxiously conjure up the spirits of the past to their services and borrow from them names, battle cries and costume in order to present the new scheme of world history in this time-honoured disguise and this borrowed language. (ibid., p. 247)

Marx's subtle entwinement of economic, political and cultural forces was largely ignored by later generations of Marxists. The major figures in the subsequent development of Marxism (Plekhanov, Lenin and Kautsky) increasingly defined Marxism as a deterministic science of inevitable historical transformation, a grand narrative which legitimated the economic and political centralisation necessary for socialism. For this first generation of Marxists, Marx's unique contribution to social science lay primarily in his analysis of the 'inner workings' of the capitalist mode of production and his identification of the 'iron laws' at work within it, laws which imposed both a structure and a direction to historical development. The relation between the 'base' and the 'super-structure' was theorised in mechanistic and functionalist terms. Thus culture was analysed as a reflection of a determining, underlying economic structure, an epiphenomenon, or 'effect', of external, material processes. And while such reductionism could be supported with reference to Marx's writings on methodology, it was viable only by ignoring the more complex analyses of the historical works.

The most frequently cited text which appears to give support to a functionalist reading of Marxism is the 'preface' to Marx's *A Contribution to the Critique of Political Economy* (1859), which advocates a strict causal relation between the economic and cultural spheres. The forces of production, Marx argues, 'constitute the economic structure of society, the real foundations on which arises a legal and political superstructure and to which correspond definite forms of consciousness. The mode of production of material life conditions the general process of social, political and intellectual life' (Marx, 1971, pp. 20–1). Culture, therefore, has no autonomy: the products of the superstructure, including ideas and consciousness, 'have no history, no development' other than as 'reflexes and echoes' of material production.

Such a standpoint suggests a functionalist model of cultural production, with its emphasis on the interrelations of parts and whole and on the ways elements of the superstructure correspond directly with the 'needs' of the base. In some of Marx's methodological formulations, culture is explained away as a residuum of a 'higher' reality or level. Marx's form of functionalist reductionism thus implies that culture has no distinctive properties but exists only as a reflection of other forces.

This functionalist reading of Marx quickly became the basis of orthodox Marxism. If the production of ideas depended on economic forces and class interests then culture itself could exercise no active role in social change. Given this canonised, functionalist interpretation of Marxism it is hardly surprising that Marxist theory failed to grasp the complexity of culture itself: within the mainstream of Marxist writings the analysis of culture became marginalised to lead a shadowy existence, an untheorised, ambiguous presence which, as we will see, lacked any analytical and substantive rigour until the work of Gramsci and the Frankfurt School.

Marx: Culture and Economic Production

Marx's sociology of capitalism contains neither a sociology of the state nor a sociology of culture, although he wrote extensively on both. In certain of his writings Marx loosely describes specific political and cultural forms as direct expressions of social and class interests produced and reproduced as functional necessities. Thus, he suggests that the art works of Leonardo da Vinci were entirely dependent 'on the state of things in Florence', while those of Raphael hinged on 'the technical advances in art made before him, by the organisation of society and the division of labour in all countries with which his locality had intercourse'. In *The German Ideology* (1846) Marx and Engels argued that the historical genesis of art flowed necessarily from developments in the division of labour and 'the conditions of human culture resulting from it'.

But such a strict functionalist, productivist analysis of both the concept of culture and cultural development is not the only model found in Marx's works. Scattered throughout his many writings is a more subtle, flexible approach in which 'superstructual elements' exercise an active and shaping role in the production and reproduction of social life. Thus in *Capital* he notes that 'Protestantism, by changing almost all the traditional holidays into work days, plays an important part in the genesis of capital' (Marx, 1957, p. 276). The so-called 'ideal' features of society actively contribute to social reproduction as material forces. Yet, as with Marx's functionalist formulations there is much vagueness and loose expression. At no point, for example, does Marx engage theoretically with the problems posed by the potential autonomy of culture, or attempt to demonstrate empirically how such autonomy might arise out of the workings of the economic and social forces of modern capitalism. Thus, writing of ancient Greek art he notes the apparent contradiction between the most backward economic structure of Greece and its 'advanced' aesthetic forms:

> As regards art, it is well known that some of the peaks by no means correspond to the general development of society; nor do they, therefore, to the material substructure, the skeleton as it were of its organisation. For example, the Greeks compared with modern [nations] or else Shakespeare. [Is] Achilles possible when powder and shot have been invented? And is the *Iliad* possible at all when the printing press and even printing machines exist? Is it not inevitable that with the emergence of the press bar, the singing and the telling and the muse cease, that the conditions necessary for epic poetry disappear? [Therefore, the difficulties lie in understanding] how Greek art and epic poetry are associated with certain forms of development [but] still give us aesthetic pleasure ... as a standard and unattainable ideal.

The problem Marx identifies is thus the apparent contradiction between the finite and historically specific nature of the 'base' and certain timeless qualities of the superstructure: Greek art, he suggests, exerts 'charm', a notion suggestive of universal and transhistorical values, a standpoint clearly at odds with Marx's materialism (Marx and Engels, 1976, pp. 83–4).

The problem of the 'partial autonomy' of culture (and art) is one Marx never resolved, and it was only in the work of later culturalist Marxists (notably Gramsci, the Frankfurt School, Lukács, Hauser and Antal) that the question of universal value and the different modes of reception were raised. Engels, in contrast, developed a more empirical approach, avoiding Marx's 'essentialism' by arguing that an 'uneven relation' necessarily subsists between the economic infrastructure and the cultural superstructure. He notes, for example, the absence of any direct links between the radical and critical philosophy of the French Enlightenment and its socio-historical context, a largely agrarian, pre-modern economic system. And writing of Ibsen he further emphasised the difficulty of attributing a direct, unmediated relationship between the modernity of Ibsen's theatre and the economically undeveloped, because of the geographically scattered Norwegian mode of production. While Engels offers a more sociological approach, it is one which avoids the problem of how is it possible for particular cultural forms to play active roles in widely differing societies and historical time. How is it possible for cultural forms to be actively effective once the mode of production on which they were genetically dependent has vanished? And if culture is more than mere 'reflexes' of 'real conditions', why is it that only certain forms survive their origins? Moreover, these forms only express 'universal' value later. What are the links, then, between their partial autonomy and the specific economic and/or social context? Marx (together with later generations of Marxists) failed to really engage with these questions, his pronouncements more elliptical than analytic. Marx's approach to the analysis of culture effectively fails to produce analytic concepts which might help to elucidate the specific nexus of economy and culture.

Thus the problem of linkages remains: Marx and Engels formulated a social theory which focussed on the interaction taking place between base and superstructure, while neglecting to specify the ways in which different contents, constituting base and superstructure, actually work. Their comments on the relation of Greek art to modern industrialism, Ibsen to the Norwegian economy and Enlightenment philosophy to French economic underdevelopment, serve only to cloud the analytical issues involved and to reinforce the view that the broad trend of a Marxist theory of culture is reductionist (culture as a reflection of the different tempos of development within a social formation). For how is it possible to reconcile the principle of autonomy with a methodological perspective which, in the main, builds on terms such as 'reflexes' and 'echoes'?

However, as I have suggested, Marx's reflections on culture, while tending towards a mechanistic, functionalist model, do contain hints of a more subtle and bold thesis. The concept of production, for example, a key element in Marx's general social theory, is not theorised solely in terms of its place in the 'base', as a crude materialist category. Production involves significant ontological and broad humanist assumptions. In discussing the human dimensions of the concept of society, Marx argues:

> We presuppose labour in a form that stamps it as exclusively human. A spider conducts operations that resemble those of a weaver, and a bee puts to shame many an architect in the construction of her cells. But what distinguished the worst architect from the best of bees is this, that the architect raises his structure in imagination before he erects it in reality ...He not only effects a change of form in the material on which he works, but he also realises a purpose of his own...(Marx, 1958, p. 178)

Thus the concept of production itself is never crudely materialistic: production always involves knowledge, thought, imagination, skills and reflexivity. Hence, although culture may reflect specific social conditions, like the reflexive nature of the architect, it contributes actively to the further development of those conditions. Without culture there is no production, for culture is not something existing externally to the 'material life process of society' but imbricated in its basic structures. Material production is productive activity which takes place within definite cultural frameworks, a process which generates the values and purposes essential for producing the 'real foundations'.

But if production always involves this cultural framework then so does politics and power. From his earliest work Marx acknowledged the revolutionary dynamic of the capitalist mode of production for shattering old illusions and traditions, transforming 'fixed and frozen' social relations into more fluid and open forms, for its essential modernity. The historical development of modern capitalism generates new institutions, new social classes and political movements. In this process culture comes to play a key role in the constitution of capitalism as a modern complex society built around inequalities of property and power. As a potentially unstable society capitalism requires some mode of legitimating ideology, a system of values which function to provide unity and social cohesion. Culture is one significant mechanism whereby capitalism might achieve the necessary degree of social integration as the basis for historical continuity. Thus, because culture may be theorised as the realm of meaning and values it is equally the realm of ideology. Without culture there is no production, and without culture there is no stability and social integration. The problem here, of course, is that such formulations are close to functionalist Marxism.

This dominant culture thesis – culture defined as ideology underpinning and legitimating bourgeois class rule – suggests a model of society held together by commonly accepted values which are derived not 'from below' but 'from above', from institutions which produce and disseminate ideology, the church, the state, education. In this argument the ruling class of modern capitalism does not rule by exercising naked force but rather through a combination of force and consent. The dominant culture thesis therefore assumes a highly centralised, holistic concept of society, one in which ideological values flow from the centre. There is thus no space for pluralism, oppositional values and an autonomous cultural sphere.

In this reductive base and superstructure model, culture is effectively swallowed up by social and economic forces, theorised as passive reflection and as ideological 'social cement'. Such a standpoint clearly assumes the existence of a coherent set of ideas located within the dominant class. As Marx and Engels expressed it in one of their most quoted formulations:

> The ideas of the ruling class are in every epoch the ruling ideas i.e. the class which is the ruling material force of society is, at the same time, its ruling intellectual force. The class which has the means of material production at its disposal has control, at the same time, over the means of mental production . . . In so far, therefore, as they rule as a class and determine the extent and compass of an epoch, it is self-evident that they do this in its whole range, hence among other things rule also as thinkers, as producers of ideas, and regulate the production and distribution of the

ideas of their age: thus their ideas are the ruling ideas of the epoch. (Marx and Engels, 1965, pp. 60–1)

However, as I have suggested above, within Marx's work there exists a more dialectical model, which challenges the concept of a unified dominant class with its coherent culture and ideology. Thus in his historical studies, Marx identified the existence of distinct fractions within the ruling class and 'cleavages' of interest which could eventuate in conflict over material resources, ideas and culture. In his studies of Bonapartism, he argued for the coexistence of competing ideas, arguing that although one set of ideas may become dominant this does not preclude the active presence of alternative and oppositional notions. For while a social class which controls material production may also control mental production, this by no means implies direct control over all culture.

Marxist Critiques of the Base–Superstructure Model

In the historical development of Marxism, Marx's caveats on the internal complexity and pluralism within advanced social formations were largely ignored. The mechanical base – superstructure model, with its emphasis on direct unmediated links between material and cultural production, dominant class and dominant ideas, was reinforced. Georg Lukács, for example, who wrote extensively on the European novel, developed a theory of realism which owed little to any complex notion of culture, but more to the economic and political ascendency of the bourgeois class. For Lukács, the rise of the bourgeoisie corresponded directly with the rise of the realist novel; the decline of this class after the 1848 revolutions, which first brought the new working-class political movement to the forefront of European politics, led inevitably to the disintegration of the realist form and its replacement by modernism. As the major aesthetic form of European literary culture, the 'progressive' realist novel successfully depicts society as a historical category while its narrative strategies portray the inherent sociality of individual personality. But with the'inevitable' decay of capitalist economic and political dominance an irrational modernism emerges (Flaubert to Kafka), with its focus no longer on the social and historical determinants of character and plot but on the asocial, fragmented, universally alienated nature of human reality.

Culture as an active mediating category effectively disappears from this historicist framework, passively mirroring the economic and political structure: Lukács's model conflates culture downwards as a reflex of the economic, thus removing any possibility of autonomy (Lukács, 1964).

Other Marxist analyses tended to follow the broad outlines of Lukács's approach, in which the unity and coherence of dominant class ideas is wildly exaggerated. However, while many of the dogmatic core assumptions remained, Marxist art historians such as F. Antal and A. Hauser did make serious attempts to develop and modify the base – superstructure model. Rejecting what they termed naïve forms of materialism, they argued that although art constituted a collective not individual phenomenon, historically bound up with society, a complex chain of intermediate links determine that aesthetic forms and styles, and thus value, increasingly become distanced from their material and/or social origins. Raising precisely the same problem as Marx in his comments on Greek art, Hauser argues that 'spiritual' achievements originate in a dialectical relationship with the economic conditions of production, a process which raises them above the status of 'mere copies' of the economic forces. The dialectical process effectively guarantees the 'triumph of the ideal'. What Hauser advocates is a refinement of the sociological method which takes account both of objective conditions and the subjective 'spirit' of the cultural producers. For both are the products of social forces but held together in a dialectical tension. Hauser was particularly concerned with the role played by the 'ideal' element in the genesis of art, seeking to relate particular cultural products both to individual psychic dispositions and the 'collective aspirations' of whole classes (Hauser, 1963, p. 274).

The question of the relation between subjective 'dispositions' and objective socio-economic conditions is clearly crucial for the development of a sociology of culture. But merely to designate the relation as 'dialectical' is to offer an empty, formalist explanation. What is the relationship, for example, between dispositions and social context, class membership, education, family, etc.? How do dispositions arise from the social conditions, and what are their distinctive properties and relation with the specifics of cultural production? Which social groups and individuals choose or select specific cultural forms as exemplars of value? And what is value? Is it historically and sociologically constituted or does it arise spontaneously out of the works themselves?

Hauser fails to deal with any of these problems. He argues that a sociology of culture based on Marxism must establish the connections between the socio-economic context and different artistic movements, because distinct art forms and stylistic trends necessarily correspond to social stratification and economic power. Art exists both in relation to the individual consciousness ('optically or orally conditioned') and as an expression of a socially conditioned class ideology.

Both Hauser and Antal were critical of the dominant ideology thesis, arguing that in most societies there existed no single dominant cultural form or style. Rather, there was pluralism of styles as different generations of artists coexist and work alongside each other, although in conflict and competition with different social classes and educational strata. Thus Hauser argues that in Italy, at Raphael's death, the Classical, Mannerist and early Baroque styles were all active, typical and relevant: 'The complexity, the tangle of interests and influences are not fully manifested in any one of the contemporary styles of that epoch' (ibid., pp. 158–9). But while advocating pluralism of styles, Hauser fails to specify the precise links between different art works and the culture, too often assuming that changes in styles correspond directly with changes in economic conditions. The result is trivial correlations and a failure to theorise the socio-cultural context adequately taking account both of the socio-economic forces and of their relations with individual or collective aspirations, values and motivation. Thus if styles depend on 'psychic' artistic dispositions, how are they related to the specific socio-cultural context? How are such dispositions formed? What is the link between individual dispositions and the collective institutional framework of society? In seeking to go beyond the base – superstructure model, Hauser has introduced a voluntaristic individualistic element, which by its nature must function in an arbitrary form, in contradiction with the collective, determining basis of social life. The relation of dispositions to the social context remains unclear, ambiguous and untheorised.

In contrast, Antal in his *Florentine Painting and its Social Background* argued for the collective and profoundly social nature of cultural production, in which culture reflected the dominant economic forces through the actions of different social classes. He suggests that the broad themes and ideas which structure individual art works correspond to the 'mentality' of a specific social class. He seeks to demonstrate how the system of patronage existing in Renaissance Florence largely determined the formal aesthetic structure of different paintings. Many of the art works were commissioned directly by wealthy patrons, merchants and bankers, and Antal analyses them as ideological representations of the social and political status of such groups. Art is thus the direct expression of ideology, produced almost automatically by the artist whose role is as a 'midwife', the medium of the broader social forces.

Given Antal's deterministic framework, how does he succeed in linking different aesthetic forms and styles to culture? Take his analysis of the paintings of the 'early Renaissance', which he argues correspond with the rise of a nascent merchant bourgeoisie (during the period 1390–1434). The characteristic artistic style of a painter such as Masaccio (1401–28) was compounded of a new and distinctive approach to the problem of space, its logical, rationalistic and 'systematic construction'. Masaccio followed the linear perspective, 'the scientific discovery of an architect, Brunelleschi', in the massive fresco he painted for the Brancacci chapel at the church of Santa Maria del Carmine. Antal notes:

> Space was now scientifically organised and logically built up through a system of perspective: an attempt was made to pass beyond merely casual, subjective observation, and to objectivise and rationalise the visual impressions. The exact science of mathematics assisted Masaccio to procure the greatest possible unity in his spatial construction, and to interrelate it in a logical manner. Every object is given its appointed place, an entirely new relationship between the figures and the landscape is built up, the old contradictory proportions are eliminated. (Antal, 1986, p. 309)

Masaccio expounded this highly rational and secular ideology in the cycle of frescoes commissioned by a rich silk merchant, Felice Brancacci, by subordinating the landscape, with its majestic, sweeping lines, to the rationalist construction of the whole work. For Antal, Masaccio's frescoes represent the highest point attained by bourgeois rationalism with its material basis anchored within the social and economic ascendency of the middle classes (Antal, 1986, p. 310). Thus the formal patterns of art express a distinctive ideology, which in Antal's analytical framework is located externally: individual painting is assimilated to class interests and class identity, and the origin and meaning of the art-work imbricated in the social composition of a distinctive social group.

Although both Antal and Hauser acknowledged the coexistence of different social groups, ideologies and artistic styles within a specific historical period and social context, and 'spiritual tendencies' which become increasingly 'tangled' and 'pervaded' by deep-seated oppositions, they tended to assimilate macro-sociological complexity and pluralism to an underlying dominant. Both Antal and Hauser, for example, employ the concept of correspondence, analysing artistic styles in their relations with social strata, and while noting pluralism at the level of social structure, arguing for the domination in any period of a specific social class. While there is great heuristic value in the macro-sociological approach to the analysis of social context, it must be rigorously analytical grasping both the complex structures and levels of social and cultural institutions. It should focus on the hierarchical nature of social–cultural formations, and distil the processes whereby the macro and micro are linked, illuminating the exact elements in this linkage. Marxist cultural historians, while paying lip-service to pluralism and internal complexity, frequently fail to deal adequately with this problem conflating micro processes with broad macro structures. Therefore the critical role of the artist, his action and values are defined passively, with the creative act the result of the workings of external social forces (Hauser, 1963, pp. 32–3).

Culture is thus theorised as the unmediated expression of class practices and interests. Culture becomes the middle term between class and society, society and art, its autonomy obscured. Clearly this presents problems for analysing such issues as the genesis of culture and the role played by agents in its construction and influence. Although these issues have been addressed by other Marxist cultural historians, too often they fail to deal adequately with the macro–micro problem. T. J. Clark, for example, arguing for the necessity to establish links between artistic form and the more general historical and social context, and explicate the process whereby the 'background' becomes the 'foreground', discovers a 'network' of real, complex relations between the two. To trace the threads which link the production of art with culture and society, analysis must focus on the highly differentiated nature of context and include such specifics as local trades, politics and entertainments, and trace how art actually 'works', shaping rather than merely reflecting social relations. In his studies of nineteenth-century French art, Clark emphasises the development of urbanism and the emergence of city spaces and new social groups all of which played key constituting roles in the genesis of modern French painting (Clark, 1973).

In much of subsequent Marxist cultural theory the assumption that art works directly express relations of class and ideology is superseded by this more 'activist' notion, in which art plays an active role in the construction of ideology and culture. The other issue remains problematic, however: how does the artist work the materials of society and culture in such a way that the background is transformed into the foreground, into art itself? At this point another form of reductionism takes place, in which the complexity of context, the micro–macro link, is transformed into the 'intentions' of artists or their creative action: 'The work of art', Max Raphael wrote, 'holds man's creative powers in a crystalline suspension from which they can again be transformed into living energies' (Raphael, 1978, p. 187). The danger here is that a Marxist determinism is supplanted by a Marxist voluntarism in which creative practice transcends the cultural context. It is maintaining the complex balance between the macro and the micro which presents one of the greatest problems for Marxist cultural theory. For Marxism, culture remained deeply problematic, and only in the work of Gramsci and the Frankfurt School was the concept theorised with any degree of rigour without lapsing into the reductionism of context or the reductionism of agent.

Gramsci: The Autonomy of Culture

Gramsci was the first major Marxist thinker to focus directly on the problems of the superstructure and raise critical questions concerning the specific relations between culture, economy, class and power. Gramsci's Marxism brought together Marx's materialism and the idealist Hegelian philosophy of the Italian thinker B. Croce: the result was a Marxism rigorously opposed to those strands of contemporary Marxist thought which classified it as a natural science of society built around the workings of specific economic and historical laws. For Gramsci, the methods employed in the natural sciences were inappropriate for a dialectical social science such as Marxism, a science concerned above all with 'consciousness' and 'praxis'. It should be stressed that Gramsci's Marxism was forged at a time when Marxism had degenerated into a quasi-religious dogma, a closed discourse impervious to issues of scientific proof and empirical evidence, a theory which had ossified into rigid rules and principles.

For Gramsci, the key to social and historical change lay outside the mechanistic model of base and superstructure, in the interrelations of distinct economic, political and ideological structures. More specifically, social change hinged on the creative role of agents engaged in 'praxis'. Sharply distinguishing his theory from 'automatic Marxism', Gramsci argued that the historical process was not the product of impersonal economic forces but the result of the workings of 'human will' organised into collective forms (trade unions, political parties, professional associations, etc.). Such collective institutions become 'the driving force of the economy effectively shaping "objective reality"' (Gramsci, 1977, p. 35).

Throughout his early writings (roughly the period from 1910 to 1921) Gramsci continually stressed the self-activity and consciousness of the working class, arguing that a fatalistic acceptance of the historical inevitability of socialism must condemn it to passivity and defensive political action. Gramsci's emphasis on will, on voluntarism, is brought out vividly in his response to the 1917 Bolshevik revolution in an article called, prophetically, 'The Revolution against *Das Kapital*'. Written shortly after the successful October revolution, Gramsci's article argued that the Bolshevik accession to power vindicated Marxism as a non-fatalistic, activist theory built around the concept of 'collective will' rather than objective 'iron laws'. Revolutionary social change was not an automatic effect of external forces acting on a largely passive mass but rather the result of a complex historical process in which a social class, becoming economically and politically dominant, will seek to establish a cultural authority over all other social classes. A 'rising class', he wrote, will necessarily strive for an 'intellectual and moral leadership', one which transcends their narrow 'corporate' interests (that is, their distinctive control of economic resources, political and social institutions) to appeal to other social strata. In this sense all revolutions are preceded 'by an intense work of cultural penetration' as the rising class strives to subjugate allied and subordinate strata to its ideas and thus its 'hegemony' (Gramsci, 1977, pp. 34–7).

Gramsci first employed the term hegemony in his *Some Aspects of the Southern Question* (1921), arguing that the proletariat 'can become the leading [dirigente] and the dominant class to the extent that it succeeds in creating a system of alliances that allow it to mobilise the majority of the working population against capitalism and the bourgeois state' (Gramsci, 1978, p. 443). A synthesis of political, intellectual and moral elements, the concept of hegemony is analytically valuable for negating the positivist theorisation of the economic as the 'basis' and culture as mere 'reflex' or 'appearance'. Hegemony points to a voluntarist component in the structure of class domination, foregrounding the active role of agents in consenting to and thus legitimising different modes of rule. Such consent, and the values which underpin it, flow from culture and cultural institutions bearing their own autonomy and reality. Culture and its institutions must exist as separate, independent elements if hegemony is to work. Gramsci's main point is that such autonomy presupposes the existence of a resilient and independent civil society, one which enables 'private institutions' such as education, political parties, trade unions and the church to function outside the control of 'political society', that is, the state. Through civil society, a dominant class will 'saturate' the institutions with the 'spirit' of its morality, traditions, and religious and political practices. A class striving for hegemony necessarily speaks for the whole of society, establishing a position from which it aims to unify and integrate.

Gramsci's contribution to the development of a Marxist theory of culture lies in his argument that in modern capitalist societies there is no longer one single class that can dominate by excluding the actions of others. A modern dominant class must listen to the voices of subordinate classes and take account of the real effects which these classes produce. Gramsci's model assumes a balance between persuasion and coercion, and although he argues for a concept of a dominant culture his work offers a more pluralist model than those of orthodox Marxism. Nevertheless, although Gramsci emphasises the role played by active consent in the legitimation of class domination, there is always involved a degree of force, control or coercion. While direct domination is linked with 'political society', the state, employing coercive measures from 'above', hegemony, as a subtle mixture of consent and coercion, flows more from 'below'. Hegemony is therefore the analytical tool for grasping the reality of moral and cultural forms without which no stable society is possible. The 'moment of hegemony' is one which always includes, alongside the economic and the political, the 'ethico-political' (Gramsci, 1978, p. 106).

Gramsci thus theorises the concept of culture in terms of an integrative process which binds the various opposing and potentially conflictual groups and classes into a unified social whole. In Gramsci's analysis, culture, as both institutions and practices, is closely bound up with history and politics, deeply imbricated in power relations. Culture is not neutral nor does it arise spontaneously from social institutions. Culture is produced by specific groups or intellectuals, especially those belonging to the 'rising class', who must combat the old and the traditional with the new and the challenging. It is these class-bound intellectuals who engage in struggles over new modes of expression, including language and popular and high culture, all of which play important roles in the forging of a new society and social relations.

One of Gramsci's most important points is that culture, while context-bound and thus finite, always involves some notion of universal values. All dominant classes, through their allied intellectuals, necessarily produce their own unique yet universal values, which form the basis of cultural hegemony. Culture is always collective, the product of collective not individual agents, and he shared with Marx the idea of contextualising culture historically. So, while 'corporate' culture is genetically and historically bound up with class and power, it transcends narrow, class, 'corporate' interests, functioning as a partly autonomous and active process. It follows that the socialist movement must of necessity go beyond challenging capitalist economics. It must generate its own distinctive *Weltanschauung* to legitimate its aspirations to cultural and political domination. The 'moment of hegemony' thus presupposes the emergence of the 'new', radical ideas about art, literature, philosophy, education and law, ideas which challenge the old and established and which carry universal claims, not class-specific ones. In this way, hegemony implies new modes of thinking about the social world, transforming social relations and the structure of society itself. Art, as one expression of the culture, is tied in with this broad process, embracing ideas about 'national feelings', 'new psychology', 'new ways of feeling', thinking and living, all of which are specific to a new social class.

It should be clear from these formulations that Gramsci is not arguing for the existence of a 'pure' class culture in which distinctive social strata transmute their economic and political interests directly into cultural forms and values. Gramsci's concept of culture transcends such a narrow and impoverished 'corporatist' perspective to embrace a position close to that developed by his Russian Marxist contemporary Leon Trotsky, who in his *Literature and Revolution* (1924) polemicised against the influential dogma of proletkult theory. Trotsky wrote his book explicitly against the theoreticians of a pure class culture who, by the early 1920s, constituted a growing influence in Soviet Marxist cultural theory.

Proletkult theory assumed a direct, unmediated link between social class and culture; all art and literature, for example, must of necessity express class interests. Trotsky opposed this reductionism by arguing that because of the proletariat's primary concern with basic economic issues and the political struggle for socialism, its involvement in day-to-day tasks militates against its developing a specific culture. The proletkult theorists defined their role as organising the needs of the proletariat, with the proletkult functioning as an organisation which consciously set out both to develop and to organise a distinctive proletarian culture.

Trotsky dismissed such a naïve and bureaucratic view:

> The bourgeoisie took power and created its own culture; the proletariat, they think, having taken power, will create proletarian culture. But the bourgeoisie is a rich and, therefore, educated class. Bourgeois culture existed already before the bourgeoisie had formally taken power. The bourgeoisie took power in order to perpetuate its rule. The proletariat in bourgeois society is a propertyless and deprived class, and so it cannot create a culture of its own. (Trotsky, 1957, ch.6)

Echoing Gramsci, Trotsky noted that as the bourgeoisie developed its wealth 'it weaned the intelligentsia to its side and created its cultural foundations (schools, universities, academies, newspapers, magazines) long before it openly took possession of the state' (ibid., p. 188). It is impossible, he concluded, to build a class culture 'behind the backs of a class'. Because of its historically subordinate role in the productive system, combined with an ingrained culture of servitude and dependence built around habit and tradition, the working class was incapable of generating a new culture before the economic and political foundations of socialist society had been laid.

Gramsci shared Trotsky's view that working-class life and consciousness was shaped largely by a combination of religious, supernatural, folkloric, profoundly conservative ideas. But while working-class culture thus lacks autonomy, characterised by 'sedimented layers' of meaning handed down from the past, it carries within it layers of ordinary, everyday common sense. Like Trotsky, Gramsci saw the role of intellectuals as the transformation of this variegated popular culture into a coherent 'world-view', one built around the possibility of socialism. Without the intervention of intellectuals the working class remains under the sway of bourgeois culture and ideology.

Gramsci described working-class culture in terms of a fragmented and contradictory ideology. Because it lacks inner coherence and the capacity to generate alternative world views, popular culture can never form the 'site' of opposition to the dominant order. Gramsci's standpoint constitutes an implicit rejection of proletkult theory as well as other contemporary Marxist analyses such as that of Ernst Bloch (who offered a far more sophisticated theory of popular culture than the proletkultists), in which popular culture was defined through an immanent utopian possibility, embodying the project of liberation from the existing society. Equally, Gramsci went beyond Trostky's orthodox Marxism, which, for all its subtleties, remained firmly tied to the Leninist principle that successful revolutions flow from working-class capture of state power through direct political struggle, to be then followed by a transformation of society and culture from the top downwards. The concept of hegemony suggests that such revolutionary optimism is insufficient to generate automatically the culture and values necessary for socialist change. Hegemony presupposes not merely the substitution of one class for another, but rather the existence of a system of alliances encompassing other social groups, which in combination enable a 'rising class' through its moral and intellectual leadership to mobilise a majority of the population. In the absence of hegemony, a structure based on the coercive role of the state will tend to dominate over society.

The concept of hegemony points to a continuing process of cultural change and development, the transformation of the old into the new, a process which goes hand in hand with changes in economics and politics. Culture, politics and revolution are a unifying process. It is not a question of building a universal culture after the revolution from the top downwards. As Trotsky put it, 'the moral grandeur of the proletarian revolution' lies in its 'laying the foundations of a culture which is above classes and which will be the first culture that is truly human' (ibid., p. 14). However, while Trotsky, like Lenin, saw culture largely in terms of the growth of science and technology, education and literacy rates, Gramsci located culture within the existing popular forms, a standpoint which links his work with that of Bakhtin (see Chapter 7). Popular culture will constitute the basis of a new, universal culture.

Culture, then, is the key to understanding Gramsci's Marxism, and the rich variety of his studies. From his prison cell in 1927 he wrote of his plans for an intense and systematic scheme of work:

> Up to now I have thought of four subjects ... Research into the formation of an Italian public spirit in the last century; in other words, research into the nature of the Italian intellectuals, their origins, their groupings according to the cultural currents of the time, their diverse modes of thought ... A study of comparative linguistics ... A study of the plays of Pirandello and the transformation in Italian theatrical taste which Pirandello represented and helped to determine ... An essay on serial stories in the newspapers, and popular taste in literature. (Gramsci, 1972, p. 9)

These four subjects, Gramsci went on, are characterised by 'a certain homogeneity', which binds them together for 'the creative spirit of the people, in its diverse phases and degrees of development underlines each in equal measure'.

Gramsci counterposed this concept of the national-popular to the folkloric-grounded popular culture of everyday life. The national-popular forms a crucial element in Gramsci's cultural theory, allowing for the re-evaluation of the diverse strands of popular culture, especially popular literature, as the potential expression of universal values, moral elements which embody 'the philosophy of the age'. Popular fiction, such as adventure stories, can generate beauty and educate readers through presenting an alternative reality to that of a dehumanising capitalist rationality and the increasingly industrialised, disciplined world of mechanised labour. Thus popular songs express a positive commitment to a social world different from that of 'official society'. The national-popular must in some way forge links with these positive strands of popular culture, and so integrate the intellectuals with the people. The fusion of these structures is exemplified in language. While all social groups employ their own distinctive language, a process of 'continual adhesion' and exchange occurs between the popular, everyday language of the people and the more refined language of the educated classes.

However, in Italy, a national-popular culture was largely absent. Intellectuals tended to form castes separated from the people, losing

20   *Cultural Theory and the Problem of Modernity*

their 'organic function' and effectively becoming the ideologues of the
ruling class. Gramsci notes, for example, that in Italy, unlike France,
Russia and Germany, the popular and national were synonomous: in
Italy the term 'national' has an ideologically very restricted meaning,
and does not in any case coincide with the 'popular', because in Italy
the intellectuals are distant from the people, i.e. from the 'nation'.
They are tied instead to a caste tradition that has never been broken
by a strong popular or national political movement from below
(Gramsci, 1985, p. 208). Thus in the work of writers such as Manzoni
and Pirandello, the people are portrayed externally, stripped of their
inner life and positive values. For this reason the Italian public turns
to the more accessible French writers, who have 'a national educative
function' through their 'close and dependent relationship between
people-nation and intellectuals', in contrast to Italian writers, who
have no sense of the people's 'needs, aspirations and feelings' (ibid.,
pp. 209–11).

So the concept of the national-popular is closely tied in with hegemony, focusing analytically on the links between different social classes
and strata (through their alliance of interests) and popular culture.
Where there exists a split between culture and the people it is owing to
the fact that the intellectuals 'have failed to represent a lay culture
because they have not known how to elaborate a modern "humanism"
able to reach right to the simplest and most uneducated classes...tied
to an antiquated world, narrow, abstract, too individualistic...' It
should not be the case that the people are excluded from so-called
'high culture' and left to folkloric notions of everyday common sense
which can be both narrow and primitive as well as creatively positive.
Gramsci dismisses the false dualism of high and popular culture other
than as ideological expressions of a rigidly hierarchical society. To
create a new culture and a new literature, it is essential 'that it sinks
its roots in the humus of popular culture as it is, with its tastes and
tendencies and with its moral and intellectual world, even if it is backward and conventional' (Gramsci, 1985, p. 102).

Gramsci's is not an idealist concept of working-class culture. Popular culture, with all its contradictions, must form part of the basis of
'high culture', which is broad and national, involving an organic
relationship between intellectuals and the people. Gramsci's concept
of culture is thus sharply distinguished from later Marxist theorists
(especially the Frankfurt School), who refuse any necessary link

between the popular and the cultural, and who increasingly divest the people of their autonomy and potential for creative action by transforming them into the passive dupes of a dominant ideology and social system. What is equally striking in Gramsci's formulations is the emphasis on the ways in which agents actively internalise cultural values, so providing legitimacy for hegemony and the subjective basis for action. And this process of internalisation occurs within specific socio-cultural institutions – education, family, political groups – and a pluralist social structure: it is not a question of dominant values annihilating all others, but of social struggles over values. Gramsci's concept of hegemony allows for 'differences' and the pluralism of other 'voices' within the structures of civil society, alternative cultures which become the site of resistance and revolution.

With its emphasis on hierarchical relations between social classes and groups and an ongoing struggle over culture, Gramsci's model of society suggests the concept of a field of forces in which the various components resist harmonious integration into the social whole, so that partly autonomous forces at work – intellectual, cultural, economic, political – constitute the context of collective class action and formation of consciousness. But while this enables Gramsci to theorise the possibility of alternative and oppositional culture and the autonomy of practices within a field of forces, his historic sense of an underlying pattern to historical development – history as an objectively unfolding process containing the possibility of universal goals of freedom – which confers meaning on action, vitiates his sociological commitment to the empirical and historically specific. Analytically, hegemony focuses on the fluid, mobile and open state of culture, on its making and remaking, on the constant shifts in the balance of forces and the living historical links between the popular and the national. Yet Gramsci's formulations suggest a closed element in which the autonomy of practices and the autonomy of culture are circumscribed by the logic of history, which points inevitably to the supercession of bourgeois hegemony by proletarian hegemony.

Chapter 2

Theorising Culture: Weber, Simmel and Social Action

Introduction

Nineteenth-century Marxist thought effectively marginalised the concept of culture assimilating it to a reductive base – superstructure model. Marxism failed to theorise the complex relation of culture to society and to spell out the complex links between cultural forms, practices and institutions and the economic and political structures. Nothing was more fateful to the study of culture than its definition of culture as 'echoes' of a real-life process, its forms corresponding directly to specific class interests and ideology. In contrast, classical sociology – Durkheim, Weber and Simmel – emerging as a distinctive discipline and differentiating itself from history, psychology, politics and economics through defining a specific object of study – society – and an appropriate methodology, engaged from its beginnings in a debate on the nature of culture.

Here the differences between sociology and Marxism are sharply articulated: rejecting the productivist model of Marxist theory in favour of a semi-culturalist model, Durkheim argued for a separate symbolic dimension to social life – collective representations such as nationalism and religion which enable individuals to communicate and establish values and meanings essential for the cohesion of modern society. It is through symbolic forms such as religion that the individual is connected with the wider society collectively sharing in experiences and beliefs. Weber, too, argued against the mechanistic view, which grounded meaning as a reflex or effect of economic-political conditions and interests, by emphasising the voluntaristic basis of meaning in social interaction. Through complex patterns of 'sociation', human agents produce threads of meaning, which then become the basis for social action. Agents do not respond passively and mechanically to external economic and material forces, but are motivated to act through their beliefs. It was the cultural not the economic sphere which generated the meanings necessary for action and thus social change.

Of all the classical sociologists it was Simmel, however, who grasped the real significance of culture for sociology, arguing that while historical materialism had theorised the role of the economic in social life, it failed to understand the complex irreducibility of culture. The task of sociology lay in constructing 'a new storey beneath historical materialism', in which culture was a major, active presence. Unlike Weber and Durkheim, Simmel and Karl Mannheim were broadly sympathetic to Marxist ideas. Indeed, it was Mannheim who, during the 1920s, suggested that a cultural sociology only became possible when the concept of culture itself became problematic, no longer regarded as an organic 'part of the immutable realm of nature' but rather as a dimension of human action, 'a sphere that people do not simply inhabit and adapt to but form themselves'. The sociological study of culture begins when culture is theorised as a distinctive realm belonging to a broader socio-historical movement and characterised specifically by the principle of autonomy.

This autonomisation of culture, the separation of culture from economics and politics, carries with it certain implications about the structure of modern society – that the social world is becoming 'decentred', that modern society has no unifying 'world view'. Here, too, lies a crucial distinction between classical sociology and Marxism. Pluralism and differentiation replace homogeneity and unity. Summing up the genesis of cultural sociology, Mannheim concluded that the social determination of cultural production becomes problematised only when social life loses its fixed and rigid forms, becoming mobile and fluid. For culture, by its very nature, is never static; culture is not, in fact, a thing or object but a process in flux, the locus of meaning and human action (Mannheim, 1982).

Rationality and the Sociology of Culture: Weber

The sociology of culture, as it developed in the work of Weber and Simmel, identified culture as a distinctive, unique realm of values, which expressed an underlying historical movement. In his studies of world religions and the role played by religious ideas in social change, Weber challenged the basic principles of nineteenth-century Marxism, that social change occurs as a direct result of an objective, material historical process operating through determining economic laws. In Weber's model, human action does not proceed automatically from the workings of specific 'material' forces but flows from a complex process involving ideas and agents motivated by cultural values. Without the ideology of Protestantism, for example, capitalism could never have developed; it was necessary for agents to internalise the values of the Protestant ethic and translate them into economic and social principles enabling action to take place. Protestant ideology constituted a specific cultural orientation to the social world, one which rejected luxury and immediate consumption in favour of the postponement of worldly gratification and the avoidance of 'all spontaneous enjoyment of life'. Protestantism embodied the ascetic 'spirit' of modern capitalism, providing the necessary ideas and motivation through which social change occurs.

In Weber's historical sociology, modern capitalism constituted a unique historical formation, one built around the rational elements of Protestantism, impersonal rules and continuous and systematic calculation and discipline. To gain salvation, Protestant theology stressed the need for 'good works' performed in this world and thus the necessity for self-discipline, an inner rationality of the personality. Systematic self-control in relation to pleasure and time was essential; the individual effectively 'supervised' his own state of grace. An 'elective affinity' existed between the norms of ascetic Protestantism and the psychological–motivational structure of capitalist values.

Weber's work therefore breaks decisively from mechanistic base and superstructure models; ideology constitutes an active element not tied to the interests of a particular social class. Ideas themselves are material, productive forces. As Weber expressed it:

> Not ideas, but material and ideal interests, directly govern men's conduct. Yet very frequently the world images that have been created by 'ideas' have, like switchmen, determined the tracks along which action has been pushed by the dynamic of interests. (Weber, 1948, p. 280)

Ascetic Protestant (especially the Calvinist sects) linked their material economic needs closely with their ideal interest in salvation. Without the two world images of Luther's concept of the 'calling' – a vocation demanding that individuals pursue worldly activity to serve God – and Calvin's notion of predestination – that everyone was destined for a place in heaven or hell and nothing could change one's fate – no action was possible. Only by following the precepts of the calling could the individual assuage the uncertainty and 'inner loneliness' that followed from predestination. By performing good works, Protestants might convince themselves they were destined for salvation; useful activity, self-control and commitment to the idea of work as an end in itself constituted the means of generating self-belief.

It was this motivational structure which was missing from orthodox Marxist accounts of social change. In Weber's sociology, culture became the key to unlock the mystery of the dynamic and specific development of Western capitalism. For only in the West was this particular form of rationality found. In India, Palestine and China the material infrastructure of capitalism also existed – markets, division of labour, money economy, trade routes – yet only in Western Europe did capitalism emerge fully out of such conditions. Weber notes, for example, that Indian geometry, natural sciences, medicine, political and historical thought, while all highly developed, lacked systematic concepts and methodology. In China science remained unorganised; there was no 'rational, systematic and specialised pursuit of science'. Moreover, the rationality which lay at the heart of Protestant culture ultimately extended itself to all spheres of social life. Modernity begins precisely with the progressive rationalisation of institutions and culture, with the breakup of a unified, dominant world-view and value system and the emergence of a pluralist structure of differentiated 'value spheres', including the political and the economic, the intellectual and the scientific, and the aesthetic and the 'erotic' (the personal sphere). Modern society is thus no longer characterised by an overarching ideology but by a network of autonomous 'fields' and competing values. This 'decentring' of the modern world implies that each sphere and its activity are judged by values inherent in it (works of art must be assessed by criteria drawn from the aesthetic sphere and not from the sphere of economics and politics, for example). Increasingly, each sphere becomes the preserve of specialists whose expert knowledge and competence enable legitimate judgements to be made.

Rationality invades the state, bureaucracy, culture, personality: the world becomes 'disenchanted', dominated by impersonal rules and regulations which govern the different spheres. Coherent and rigorously systematic ideas replace the irrational, magical elements characteristic of pre-modernity (Weber, 1948, p. 328).

Clearly Weber's cultural sociology challenged many of the basic assumptions of Marxist theory: the principle of differentiated, distinctive and unique spheres suggesting that the expansion of autonomy in relation to politics, culture, law and morality develops independently of direct class and economic interests. Weber emphasised that a systematic application of impersonal rules and regulations to the whole range of social life including architecture, mathematics, science and music was characteristic of Western culture. In his unfinished study of the sociology of music, *The Social and Rational Foundations of Music* (1912), he attempted to demonstrate that Western music, once it had achieved autonomy with the weakening of various forms of patronage, embodied the rational principles of harmony, polyphony and counterpoint. Modern musical notation further facilitated the wider transmission of musical performance but with limited scope for 'irrational' improvisation. Furthermore, the invention of specific musical instruments formed the necessary material basis for the progressive rationalisation of Western music: non-Western cultures, for example, had no equivalents for the piano, violin and organ. Music, as a distinctive sphere, thus develops both internally (the rational structure of musical form)and externally (the specific social and economic conditions) (Weber, 1978).

Although Weber's Eurocentric concept of rationality ultimately weakens his general argument (Eastern cultures generated different but musically valid forms of rationality, together with equivalent musical instruments), his fundamental approach to the sociology of culture sets itself against those reductionist approaches which linked economic and class interests directly with forms of cultural production. To explain complex cultural phenomena adequately it was essential both to explore the external determinate (the technical refinement of specific musical instruments, for example) and internal, formal properties (systematic tone intervals and notation) and to grasp both as material forces. Weber was especially hostile to crude materialist analyses of art and culture, which he linked with Marxism. At the German Sociological Association Conference (1910) devoted to the subject of 'Technology and Culture' he criticised all attempts to make direct links between aesthetic forms and technology. Rather, the links between aesthetic forms and culture were indirect, mediated by human experience and technology:

> But...we ask whether modern technology does not stand in any relation to formal-aesthetic values; the answer in my opinion is undoubtedly affirmative. This is so in so far as wholly specific formal values in our modern artistic culture could only be born due to the existence of the modern city with its tram-lines, underground, electrical and other lights, shop-windows, concert halls and restaurants... the whole wild dance of tone and impressions of colour, the interwoven sensations of sexual fantasy and the experiences of variants of the psychic make-up...I believe that wholly specific values of modern painting could not be perceived, since their attainment would not have been possible by people who [had not experienced] the teeming masses, the night lights and reflexes of the modern city with its means of communication...it is clearly impossible in my opinion that certain formal values of modern painting could ever have been achieved without the particular impression made by the modern metropolis – a spectacle never seen before in history – powerful by day but overwhelming by night. (Whimster and Lash, 1987, pp. 279–80)

Weber was one of the few sociologists aware of the complex ways modern culture becomes transmuted into aesthetic images, and while his analysis is remarkably close to the work of Simmel and Benjamin (see pp. 32–6; 90–1) its importance lies more in attempting to ground these processes within a theory of the development of autonomous value spheres, the differentiation of 'life orders', with each characterised by specific internal values. There is no longer a single, overarching world view or ideology which functions to unify and integrate the social world, as was the case in pre-modern societies, but rather a pluralistic and decentred culture in which there are neither universal values nor certainty but scepticism and value relativism.

Culture and the Principle of Autonomy

Weber's value spheres – the political and the economic, the intellectual and the scientific and the erotic and personal – are autonomised in the course of social development. Each sphere has its own internal logic and remains independent from the others. Weber was quite clear on the follies of mixing the separate spheres or reducing them to a single dominant element such as the mode of production. In 1919, for example, he defended the Bavarian playwright, Ernst Toller, against the charge of treason brought by the German state for his part in the abortive communist uprising in Munich. In his fusion of revolution, political and artistic values, Toller had failed to understand the irreducible pluralism of the modern world. For Toller, love, politics and art were one:

> Art is no longer a flight from life, but life itself. In the hugely powerful class struggle of the proletariat there glows the divine spark of pleasure, which lights the way out of a society of misery and chance to the work of art of the new society.

Although Weber had little sympathy for such sentiments, he defended Toller because of Toller's integrity, his principles and convictions and his failure to fully understand the consequences of his actions. Toller, he argued, actually knew nothing about economics, politics or socialism: 'God in his wrath chose Toller to be a politician' (Dahlmann, 1987).

Toller's rejection of pluralism, his attempted synthesis of politics with art predate the politically committed drama of Bertolt Brecht, whose fundamental principle of epic theatre, that drama forms an integral part of the class struggle, awakening the individual's awareness of the economic and political forces at work in society, clearly runs against the grain of Weber's cultural modernity. Brecht's fusion of politics, economics and culture, with its concept of art as a form of practice seeking to transform society, represents a standpoint consciously opposed to the principles of autonomy and 'disinterestedness'.

The strength of Weber's position lies in the implicit rejection of the ideological cultural politics practised by totalitarian regimes such as fascism and communism, in which art and aesthetics become stripped of all vestiges of autonomy and the boundaries between culture and society are fatally eroded. Nevertheless, Weber's model of cultural differentiation poses serious problems for the sociology of culture: pluralism has the effect of collapsing culture into 'network' concepts and severing it from power and power relations. In contrast, the Marxist Gramsci analysed culture as partly autonomous yet always imbricated in the structure of economic and class forces: culture was both a 'higher sphere' and yet one based in relations of power. Weber's spheres seem to float above the specifics of society, observing an ideal internal logic unaffected by the events, practices and structures in the external world.

In his studies of the genesis of modern culture, Weber had linked his broad historical theme of the progressive rationalisation of the European world with the 'internal rationality' of the human personality, its continuous, systematic self-control and discipline as the basis of social development. Such formulations, however, while critiquing Marxist positivistic materialism, suffer from an excess of idealism at the expense of materialism. Thus while Weber theorises culture in terms of action, meaning and social bonds, of the ways in which agents produce and act on meanings, the differentiation thesis remains too abstract and ahistorical. It fails to provide analytical concepts or categories which can link culture with other elements of society and, more significantly, it lacks historical specificity. What is the time-span for Weber's spheres? Are these spheres always tied in with modernity? And if so are they always autonomous? In Renaissance Florence, for example, distinctive spheres emerged which strove to establish their autonomy precisely through their internal logic and specialised practices. Nevertheless, spheres such as the aesthetic maintained close links with economic production and political patronage. Michael Baxandall, for instance, has shown that fifteenth-century Florentine painters were equally active in both the commercial and the artistic spheres, so that the widespread practice of gauging containers, barrels for example, shaped the ways artists perceived and represented natural objects. The skills necessary for the correct gauging of barrels were highly specialised, yet the painter Piero della Francesca produced a mathematical handbook written specifically for merchants:

> The skills that Piero or any painter used to analyse the forms he painted were the same as Piero or any commercial person used for surveying quantities. And the connection between gauging and painting Piero himself embodies is very real. On the one side, many of the painters, themselves business people, had gone through the mathematical secondary education of the lay schools: this was the geometry they knew and used. (Baxandall, 1988, p. 87)

Rather than the development of autonomous, internally regulated spheres, this example suggests partly autonomous, overlapping structures (or fields) as the chief characteristic of cultural development.

Although Weber's differentiation thesis is valuable for locating the autonomy principle at work within historical and cultural development, it tends to separate the independence of structure from its dependent relation on the broader social forces. Theorising culture as a distinctive realm governed by its own specific principles is characteristic of later sociologists such as Parsons and Habermas. However, focusing on the internalist nature of culture runs the risk of severing it from the historical process, conceiving the autonomy principle as an automatic product of a necessary differentiation process. The autonomy of culture is not given: it must be made by a combination of individual and collective action. Above all, the autonomy principle must not be transformed into ahistorical abstractions, but grounded in historical specificity.

Simmel: Modernity and the Tragedy of Culture

Of all the classical sociologists, it was Georg Simmel who made the problem of modern culture the centre of his sociological studies. Simmel published widely on art and literature (Dante and Rodin, for example) and analysed the new phenomena of trade exhibitions, Alpine travel, the changing role of women and sexuality in modern culture, the significance of fashion and the bewildering plurality of styles characteristic of modernity. But his major contribution to a sociology of culture was his *Philosophy of Money* (1900), a work which played a key role in the studies of reification and culture carried out some years later by Georg Lukács and the Frankfurt School.

Like Weber, Simmel defined the subject matter of sociology as forms of social interaction between active human agents, the structure of such sociation involving complex cultural meanings. Simmel rejected the positivist argument that society constituted an objective, external system dominating its members. Rather, society was conceived in relational terms as an intricate web of multiple interactions. Simmel opposed psychological explanations for social action, arguing that sociology was essentially concerned with 'reciprocal affirmation', the ways whereby individuals relate to each other's action and conduct. Above all, Simmel sought to avoid what he considered the false totalisation of society made by Marxism. Society was not a thing or a system built around objective laws of economic development, but a complex 'labyrinth' involving the ceaseless interaction of many elements:

Society is not the absolute entity which must first exist so that all the individual relations of its members – super-and sub-ordination, cohesion imitation, division of labour, exchange ... can develop within its framework or be represented by it; it is only the synthesis or the general term for the totality of these specific interactions. Any one of the interactions may, of course, be eliminated and 'society' still exist, but only if a sufficiently large number of others remain intact. If all interaction ceases there is no longer any society. (Simmel, 1990, p. 175)

In opposition, then, both to sociological positivism and mechanistic Marxism, Simmel sought to recover the concept of society as the product of socially mediated human action, arguing that traditional sociology had tended to ignore the 'real' life of society as 'we encounter it in our experience'. Simmel's task lay in examining the 'microscopic molecular' social processes, the invisible threads woven between individuals, laying bare the hidden relationships that constitute sociation or interaction. The focus was on micro-sociological investigation of such significant social relationships as the dyad, secret societies and social gatherings such as balls and parties. Nevertheless, although critical of the holistic tendency of Marxism, Simmel clearly regarded his own contribution as a supplement, not an alternative, to Marx's historical social theory, constructing

a new storey beneath historical materialism such that the explanatory value of the incorporation of economic life into the causes of intellectual culture is preserved, while these economic forms themselves are recognised as the result of more profound valuations and currents of psychological, even metaphysical preconditions. (Simmel, 1990, p. 56)

In *The Philosophy of Money,* Simmel provides an exhaustive 'phenomenological' analysis of the social and cultural significance of money in modern industrial society. In an early essay, 'Money in Modern Culture' (1896) he had criticised historical materialism for making 'the entire cultural process dependent on economic conditions', arguing that the 'ultimate source' of cultural life was not material production but metaphysical, 'a divine secret' (Simmel, 1991). However, although the origins of culture may be shrouded in mystery the specific culture of modernity is described in Weberian terms as differentiation and autonomisation. The process of differentiation has the effect of necessarily separating the individual from the world of objects, so promoting cultural pluralism and the emergence of distinct and autonomous cultural forms. But cultural modernity is more than the mere expansion of autonomy: there is a dialectical twist to the tale as cultural forms are transformed from artefacts which express human activity and values into external facts and things which are separate from human action and value. Thus the development of modern culture leads increasingly to alienation and the fragmentation of social and personal life.

The Culture of Modernity

Anticipating the Frankfurt School's critique of mass society and culture, Simmel noted how new technologies of production generate consumerism and a society in which 'modern man' becomes surrounded by a mass of cultural objects. Modern culture tends to a levelling process in which the inner value of cultural objects 'suffers under the uniform convertibility of the most heterogeneous elements into money'. What Simmel called the 'tragedy of culture' is precisely this tendency to reduce everything to one level, 'the rational, calculating nature of modern times against the more impulsive, holistic, emotional character of earlier epochs' (Simmel, 1991, p. 28).

Modernity is thus theorised by Simmel in terms of a tension between the rapid development of science, technology and objective knowledge and the erosion of subjective, personal culture. 'Every day and from all sides', he wrote, 'the wealth of objective culture increases, but the individual mind can enrich the forms and contents of its own development only by distancing itself still further from that culture...' The result is an external and impersonal culture built on quantitative, monetary relations (ibid., pp. 446–8). Writing on the Berlin Trade Fair of 1896, Simmel noted that with the increasing specialisation in the field of production a more differentiated mode of consumption compensates for the individual's 'one-sided and monotonous role in the division of labour'. Here Simmel's analysis is superficially close to Marx's critique of capitalist social relations, with its emphasis on the transfer of labour power into a commodity objectively separate from the worker. 'The differentiation of the active side of life is apparently complemented through the extensive diversity of its passive and receiving side' (Simmel, 1991, p. 120). In a culture characterised by restless, unrelenting, feverish activity, the 'core of meaning slips through our fingers' (ibid., p. 23).

Thus culture, the realm of meaning and purposes, becomes externalised, and in his famous essay on urbanism Simmel described the gap developing between the immense culture of modernity embodied in material things, and the individual's limited capacity for knowing and understanding this process. Simmel identified the division of labour as the institution responsible for reducing the human agent to 'a negligible' quantity unable to relate in any meaningful way to objective culture, increasingly becoming 'a mere cog in an enormous organisation of things and powers which tear from his hands all progress, spirituality and value in order to transform them from their subjective form into the form of purely objective life' (Simmel, 1950, p. 442). Therefore although the culture of modern society enables the individual to play a variety of roles and to participate in more variegated social groups than did pre-industrial culture – the individual is no longer so immersed in kinship and narrow occupational structures which inhibit personal development and the growth of individuality – this shift from cultural homogeneity to cultural differentiation is wrought at great cost. The objectification of culture based on increasing specialisation generates estrangement between the subject and its products, the 'sheer quantity' of the objects produced confronting the individual as external, autonomous entities: 'Cultural objects increasingly evolve into an interconnected enclosed world that has increasingly fewer points at which the subjective soul can interpose its will and feelings' (Simmel, 1990, p. 46).

On one level, therefore, Simmel advanced the view that social development necessarily leads to a decentred culture characterised by multiple participation in a complex of social circles. But as modern society becomes institutionally decentred, culture becomes increasingly rationalised and money, with its 'colourless and indifference' the basis of all value: quantitative values replace qualitative ones, the world is structured through mathematical formulas, social life dehumanised by 'stable and impersonal' time schedules; punctuality, calculability and exactness pervade all spheres of cultural life. Everyday life itself comes to be dominated by the principles of rational 'continuous mathematical operations'. Thus the tension between objective and subjective culture is exacerbated by the development of the division of labour and a money economy. The crisis in modern culture lies in the logic of modernity, which transforms the creative subject into a passive object, reifying the products of human culture and effectively eliminating purposive human action.

Simmel employed the term 'tragedy of culture' to describe this process of cultural differentiation and 'unfolding multiplicity', which makes 'subjective culture' (the inner state of the self as embodied externally in the artefacts of aesthetic production) deeply problematic:

> Thus, the typically problematic situation of modern man comes into being: his sense of being surrounded by an innumerable number of cultural elements which are neither meaningless to him, nor in the final analysis, meaningful. In their mass they depress him, since he is not capable of assimilating them all, nor can he simply reject them since, after all, they do belong potentially within the sphere of his cultural development. (ibid., p. 186)

The tragedy lies in the inability of modern humanity to successfully assimilate material objective culture into subjective individual expression. But what does such 'objectification' mean for the individual? Does the world of modern culture constitute an external reality or structure 'out there', which imposes itself on the individual? Or is it rather that the objective artefacts of culture become meaningful only when the agent has internalised and assimilated them successfully to his or her consciousness? Simmel's analysis of the cultural rationality and the increasing penetration of the money economy into social life suggests a homologous relation between the fragmentary and fleeting experiences of everyday life and the failure of culture to provide a higher unifying purpose. Simmel introduced the concept of 'the pathos of distance' to further explicate the complex dialectic of culture. His main argument is that the human subject grasps the nature of reality only by stepping back from the cultural objects which constitute reality. A money economy, especially in an advanced capitalist form, develops this sense of distance (for example, the expansion of credit transactions, which reduce the personal and psychological immediacy of monetary exchange). Cultural development is thus structured around apparently irreconcilable contradictions: the source of Simmel's cultural pessimism lay in his argument that subjective culture, with its rich inner life, must necessarily have its basis in cultural objectification. Only then can the human potential for creativity be realised.

Such a thesis, however, is both too abstract and non-historical, the tragedy of culture subsumed under a general law of differentiation. The deterministic and fatalistic perspective is clear: the division of objective and subjective culture into a permanent feature of modernity constitutes an extrapolation of a particular tendency within modern culture to transform cultural artefacts into commodities, and for market and commercial criteria to invade the cultural sphere. Simmel's sociology of culture never examines the relations of production in any systematic detail: the fetishism of commodities (Simmel's objectification of culture) represents a special case of the contents of culture, but it cannot be analysed as the dominant element. The specifics of cultural development are far more complex and variegated than Simmel's abstract model suggests. As the Marxist cultural theorist Sigfried Kracauer noted, Simmel's analyses exist outside historical time and also, one might add, they lack adequate contextual grounding. Simmel's sociology of culture is a philosophical and not a sociological critique, a 'metanarrative' in which the concept of 'life' functions as the mainspring of culture and its 'surging dynamism' (Frisby, 1985, p. 119).

Simmel developed no specific concepts for the analysis of culture: distance, tragedy, fragmentation and reification form part of a broad critique in which one element is isolated and built into the status of a general law. Thus there is no space for alternative modes of action, no awareness of culture as an element in social struggles and opposition to the existing power relations. The links between the different forms of cultural production are theorised so abstractly that the rich variety of cultural forms and institutions float free of specific social and historical contexts. Simmel never poses the question of how culture changes and which elements are involved in such change. The specific genesis of a cultural form is ignored, and it is surprising that such lacunae have not detracted from current attempts to raise Simmel as a major figure in cultural sociology. Yet, in analysing cultural forms – whether the paintings of Rembrandt or trade fairs – Simmel fails to place them within a specific framework of cultural production, nor does he seek to disclose the links between the artefacts and other features of society. Simmel's cultural sociology remains trapped within traditional approaches to aesthetic issues and fails to break decisively from highly individualistic methodology and analysis. The false antinomy of subjective and objective culture has the effect of eliminating the communicative basis of culture and the ways in which, through the production of meanings and values, individuals relate to one another.

An insufficiency of materialism characterises Simmel's cultural theory. No explanation is offered for the genesis of cultural forms, and the historical dimension is too abstractly rendered. Simmel's microscopic analyses exist at the expense of the broader, macro structures. His ambition to create 'a new storey' beneath that of historical materialism is fatally flawed: for theorising culture only within the framework of the superstructure breaks its living relation with those agents and institutions that produce and reproduce it contextually. Durkheim noted Simmel's tendency to reduce the field of sociological research to 'extreme indeterminateness', in which the boundaries fluctuate according to 'arbitrary judgement' and 'individual temperament'. Simmel raises problems unrelated to determinate categories of fact: they are general themes for philosophical meditation. And, anticipating Simmel's appeal to later postmodern sociology, with its elision of boundaries and lack of rigorous methodology, Durkheim concludes: 'As the spirit moves him the questions with which he deals because of their very imprecision, expand or contract' (Durkheim, 1982, p. 193).

Chapter 3

Problems of Culture Industry

I have argued that Gramsci's contribution to a Marxist theory of culture implied both a concept of field of forces or 'force field', in which opposing social groups strive for domination and legitimacy, and a notion of 'collective agent', whose practices structure the social world. Culture was historical, political and institutional functioning at both the ideological and action levels. Through Gramsci's theorisation of culture as partially autonomous, it became possible to grasp the rich complexity of 'hegemony' allowing for a space in which subordinate groups critically internalised the values of the dominant class while simultaneously generating alternative values essential for social action.

In sharp contrast to Gramsci's voluntarism, a more deterministic and politically pessimistic Marxist theory of culture became elaborated in the critical theory of the Frankfurt School. The main focus of critical theory became the problem of social integration and the role played by the emerging mass media and mass culture in the maintenance of social order. While Gramsci's work has been described as belonging to the so-called 'Western Marxist' tradition (including the Frankfurt School, Lukács, Bloch and Benjamin), because of its emphasis on the constituting role of culture in the genesis of historical formations and social change (as distinct from the 'economism' of Soviet Marxism), this can be a profoundly misleading view. For Gramsci's Marxism is based on the principle of historical specificity and the capacity of the working class to transform society. The role played by intellectuals was crucial: it was not, as it became with the Frankfurt School, a question of intellectuals providing a 'critique' of an exploitative, highly rationalised capitalism, but rather of their establishing connections between the popular culture and consciousness and the process of revolutionary social change. But although the analysis of culture formed the key element in both the Frankfurt School's and Gramsci's Marxism, the broad theoretical perspective of Western Marxism encompassed a concept of theory as 'critique' and not as a science of capitalist civilisation and culture, a philosophical standpoint built around such humanist notions as praxis, alienation, emancipation and utopia. Thus although the Frankfurt School analysed the economic and political problems of modern capitalism (more especially in the work of F. Neumann and F. Pollock), the focus was not primarily on establishing a historical sociology of social formations, on developing empirical studies of the complex class structures of modern societies and the different forms of social struggles, or on elucidating the possible laws regulating economic and social change.

From the beginning, critical theory distinguished itself from all forms of positivism (or what Max Horkheimer called traditional theory) through its emphasis on the unfinished, incomplete nature of the social process and on aiming to disclose its immanent, hidden tendencies (the potentiality for human emancipation and freedom):

> By defending the endangered and victimised potentialities of man against cowardice and betrayal, critical theory is not to be supplemented by a philosophy. It only makes explicit what was always the foundation of its categories: the demand that through the abolition of previously existing material conditions of existence the totality of human relations be liberated. (Marcuse, 1968, p. 145)

For critical theory there was no objectively given world made up of 'facts', but forms of knowledge mediated historically through praxis and oriented towards possibility and change.

Methodologically, the Frankfurt School attacked the reductionism of orthodox Marxism, arguing for the relative autonomy of the different 'spheres' which constituted society, especially the political and cultural. The Hegelian concept of totality was the key to understanding both the historical process and the structure of society. All elements of the social whole are linked together through contradictions while preserving their relative autonomy from the economic structure. In this sense, all facts could be conceived as elements of a broader whole, which combined the 'particular' and the 'universal', so that, for example, while the division of labour objectively constituted a specific occupational structure embracing collective social labour, it equally expressed universal human interests linked with emancipation and freedom from necessity.

With its emphasis on the superstructure, Western Marxism clearly owed far more to Hegel's idealist philosophy than to Marx's materialist ontology. History, for example, was theorised in terms of an objective *telos* embracing the ultimate goal of human freedom. But this historical goal was not predicated on specific analyses of the forces and relations of production, on contradictions within particular modes of production, but couched rather from the standpoint of a philosophical critique of culture. For these reasons a work such as Ernst Bloch's *The Spirit of Utopia* (1920) constitutes an exemplary text of Western Marxism for its idealised, totalising, messianic view of culture which, under the impress of modern capitalism, had become fragmented and dehumanised. Describing his Marxism as belonging to the 'warm stream' (humanist and emancipatory) as distinct from the 'cold stream' (scientific, economically deterministic), Bloch stressed the immanent openness of social reality, a rich and complex potential not dependent on the workings of Marx's so-called 'iron laws' and historical necessity.

Bloch's major concept, the 'not yet', opposed the rigid notion of a predetermined future while remaining firmly rooted in social and historical reality, for any possible future must be grounded in the social and historical process. The 'not yet' is an implicit presence within the existing reality, its potential realised through human action. And it is culture which provides the basis for social change. As cultural forms develop they tend to outstrip their material foundations, leading to what Bloch calls a 'cultural surplus' which finds expression in utopian hopes and longings, ideas and aspirations embodied in literary and artistic genres (including fairy stories), in carnivals and in dreams.

The principle of hope was thus firmly rooted in utopia. Bloch criticised Marx for denigrating the concept and tradition of utopia in favour of a scientific Marxism and materialism in which the goal of socialism becomes a narrow utilitarianism, for example, an expanding consumerism. Describing such a position as 'red philistinism', Bloch proposed that utopia and Marxism, far from opposing each other were necessarily complementary. Utopia formed the realm of desire and the basis of human action, while Marxism generated knowledge and social analysis. Bloch would have warmed to Oscar Wilde's dictum that 'a map of the world that does not include Utopia is not even worth glancing at for ... Progress is the realisation of Utopias' (Wilde, 1955). For the creative strength of utopian thought lay in his emphasis on the creative role of the human agent. Utopia opposed the dominant tendency of capitalism to transform culture from a living process into an inert realm of things and objects, reducing the individual to a passive product of the historical process. Utopia humanises history and nature by freeing the 'here and now' into purposive action bound to the ideal of a classless society centred on the principles of emancipation and freedom.

Perhaps the core of Bloch's Marxism, its Hegelian legacy, was his belief in the immanent purposiveness of history, its actuality grounded in an integrated utopian whole which successfully supersedes the incomplete fragmentary 'not yet' of capitalist culture. It is this concept of utopian possibility which exercises a critical role in Frankfurt School cultural theory. Bloch rejected any form of Marxism which situated social transformation within a rigid sequential series, arguing that such a 'mechanistic standpoint' narrows and diminishes reality. The goal of Marxism was not a positivistic science based in the workings of inevitable economic laws, but rather the elucidation of society as made and remade through human praxis. This is the standpoint of Lukács who, in works such as *History and Class Consciousness* (1923), stressed the method of cultural critique over historical, socio-economic analysis. And influenced by the pessimistic cultural sociology of Georg Simmel, both Lukács and Bloch grounded truth in a supra-historical process and the privileged ontology of the universal class, the proletariat. More specifically, the idea of culture as an organic, integrated whole increasingly fragmented by the onset of industrial capitalism and modernity became one of the dominating themes of both theorists' Marxism.

The Dialectic of Culture

In sharp contrast, the theorists of the Frankfurt School (notably T. W. Adorno, M. Horkheimer, H. Marcuse) while assimilating the concepts of utopia and historical immanence, rejected the idea of culture as an integrated whole. Adorno was especially critical of Lukács's and Bloch's nostalgic theorisation of the past, an idealised view of culture derived not from Marx but from nineteenth-century philosophies of history in which culture functioned as the expression of the whole of society or civilisation; or from the new science of anthropology, which conceived culture as 'a whole way of life' culture as ordinary involving rituals, social values, institutions. Equally, Adorno criticised theories which identified culture with 'spiritual well-being' or linked it exclusively with the arts. But he rejected particularly, as a false antinomy, Lukács's mythical, pre-capitalist integrated culture and its fragmented, fractured, alienated modern form. Lukács had supposed a necessary and direct link between economic production and culture, arguing that with increasing capitalist crises culture itself becomes problematic: as capitalism declines so must culture. Such reductionism failed to grasp that it was precisely the capitalist mode of production which enabled culture to free itself from external pressures and institutional constraints to fulfil its promise of autonomy.

In pre-capitalist society, culture was tied to economic, political and religious authority, although it struggled against such powerful forces. The eighteenth and nineteenth centuries witnessed the emergence of new social groups, social classes and social institutions, independent of traditional modes of patronage and state control (what the Frankfurt School theorists term 'the public sphere') in which culture and cultural production established a genuine autonomous sphere. This slowly developing process of the autonomisation of culture leads to a more critical and dialectical relation between the different forms of cultural production and society. Once culture has established its own, unique sphere (even though it may not attain complete autonomy), its values are no longer those of its patrons or of the market-place, nor of the wider capitalist system and its political culture, but belong rather to a universal, humanist and emancipatory logic. Culture becomes 'oppositional', a 'protest' against the dehumanising logic of capitalist economy. Culture thus comes to express values, hopes and aspirations which run counter to the existing reality.

This 'affirmative culture', the legacy of the 'bourgeois epoch', is built on what Marcuse calls 'spiritual values' and is fundamentally idealist: 'To the need of the isolated individual it responds with general humanity, to bodily misery with the beauty of the soul, to external bondage with internal freedom, to brutal egoism with the duty of the realm of virtue' (Marcuse, 1968, p. 98). Although this affirmative culture was defined by Marcuse, it was left to Adorno to ground it historically. Its empirical forms exist only within the framework of modern capitalist societies in which social inequality, hierarchies, power and social status challenge the autonomy and promise of culture. For Adorno, culture develops only through its necessary historical relation with the 'life process of society', but its immanent universality inevitably drives it into conflict with that society.

The relation of culture to economy is dialectical: as capitalism generates the structural basis for the autonomisation of culture allowing it to realise its promise and be 'true' to itself, forces are simultaneously unleashed which prepare the ground for cultural disintegration. Adorno's subtle dialectical thrust suggests that the threat to culture flows directly from those elements, making for its potential autonomy.

One of the major concepts in the Frankfurt School analysis of culture, the public sphere, was used extensively by Horkheimer to refer to those cultural instutions (notably education and the media) in which the bourgeois class succeeded in organising the structure of public information and debate, and aimed to institutionalise the democratic control over state activities. The growth of the public sphere corresponded closely with the emergence of a distinct bourgeois class striving for political dominance over pre-bourgeois institutions and culture. However, the broad tendency of capitalism to develop highly centralised economies and polity has the effect of producing collectivist ideologies in conflict with the liberal ideology of the public sphere. The emphasis is no longer on the concept of the autonomous individual but on a general conformity to the prevailing norms of existing society. The idea of the autonomous individual, wrote Horkheimer, 'did not survive the process of industrialisation, and human relationships tend to a point wherein the rule of economy over all personal relationship ... turns into a new and naked form of command and obedience' (Horkheimer, 1972). For Horkheimer, the family, once the centre in the process of the socialisation of individuals, loses its educational and cultural functions as individuals are increasingly socialised by external institutions: the result is the diminuition of humanity, with individuals becoming mere cogs in a machine and reflective thought and free time being assimilated to the dehumanised norms of bureaucratic organisation and administration.

The economic and political logic of capitalism leads inevitably to the eclipse of the public sphere. The social structure of modern capitalism is no longer characterised by strong, independent institutions which guarantee individual values and freedom. The autonomous individual disappears. A new mode of social integration arises, based on the concept of 'culture industry', a structure organised collectively around capitalist economic principles, a highly rationalised system of cultural production which effectively socialises individuals into a state of passivity and conformism. Culture industry develops out of the ruins of the public sphere for with the growth of cartels, monopolies and the elimination of genuinely free competition, the core institutions of modern capitalism provide no space for autonomy and freedom. Bureaucracy, rationality and administration dominate society: the public sphere shrivels and an atomised social structure replaces the structured pluralism of bourgeois affirmative culture.

The transition from public sphere to culture industry involves an important 'instrumental' role for science: the scientistic, anti-humanist principles of bourgeois science permeate society as a whole, leading inexorably to a new mode of domination centred on technology and bureaucracy. For the Frankfurt School, an 'instrumentalist' form of rationality, one based on the principles of calculation and utility, saturates all forms of culture and social life; instrumental or formal rationality (the terms derive from Max Weber) is largely concerned with the efficient functioning of existing society, with the here and now of organisations and limited goals. In contrast, 'substantive rationality' is primarily concerned with 'ultimate questions', a rationality which focusses on the possibilities which human society possesses to realise human freedom and justice and a social life governed by universal values. Culture industry (a term which covers films, television, books, magazines, newspapers, sport and leisure) works through instrumental reason and represents the negation of the substantive rationality of Enlightenment philosophy, with its belief in reason conquering the social world for the advance of all humanity. Consciousness thus becomes alienated from the realm of purposive action, critical values and practice. Increasingly, the relations between individuals tend towards relations between things analogous with the structure of commodities in the wider society. In societies dominated by culture industry, untruth, writes Adorno, permeates every form of cultural communication (Adorno, 1991, p. 90).

Culture Industry and the Case of Music

In modern society culture comes to lose its critical function. It no longer affirms truth through resisting the formal rationality of the 'administered world', but increasingly comes under the influence of the law of commodification. A split develops between the 'higher spheres' of culture (modernism, the avant-garde), which resist commodification, and the 'lower spheres' (the product of culture industry), which tend to follow the law of commodity exchange. In his essay 'Culture and Administration', Adorno argued that once culture has come under the sway of formal, instrumental rationality it is planned and administered in ways which damage it irreparably. The norms which govern culture are not those intrinsic to it but are imposed externally. (Adorno, 1991, Ch. 4)

The theory of culture industry, first elaborated in Adorno and Horkheimer's *Dialectic of Enlightenment* (1944), has often been interpreted as a deeply pessimistic intellectual response of a group of exiled cultural élitists who had been forcibly transplanted from a traditional European culture to one based entirely on commercial principles. The American popular media, especially the radio and fiction, were dominated by the techniques of mass production and the targeting of homogeneous mass publics, tendencies largely undeveloped in contemporary European culture. However, to situate the theory of culture industry within a specific social context is to ignore its wider ramifications as a structure integral to capitalist societies with varying traditions and history. Moreover, culture industry does not restrict itself solely to the spheres of popular art-forms, nor does it necessarily draw a false antinomy between high and popular culture. In his early studies of Wagner, for example, Adorno traced the origins of culture industry to the latter half of the nineteenth century and specifically to the realm of 'high culture' itself. He notes that the historical context of culture industry was the commercialised mass culture associated with the new forces of mass circulation newspapers and magazines, the emergence of popular theatre and popular song, the mass production of cheap fiction. But equally and paradoxically, the inherent principles of mass culture can be found in the work of those modern artists, such as Wagner, who searched for the ideal of 'pure art' or 'pure music'.

Wagner conceived his operas as the 'art works of the future', the culmination of aesthetic culture uniting into a self-contained whole the different worlds of music, theatre and painting, and demanding from his audience total commitment. Wagner's operas were no mere passive entertainment, music and spectacle designed for a pleasure-seeking bourgeois public; for only art freed from its dependence on bourgeois culture was autonomous. But Wagner, argues Adorno, was mistaken: his operas exemplify the essential features of the culture industry. Wagner devalues the individuality of the characters in terms of the whole; the historical dimension disappears in favour of a 'spatialisation' of time and the assimilation of historical context to myth; sound drowns out all harmony, which, combined with an insistence on spectacle, demands a passive audience able to grasp meaning and structure through the endless repetition of leitmotiv. More specifically, Adorno argued that by creating an illusion of a real world based in myth, prehistory and the archaic, Wagner succeeded in transforming the real historical world of industrial capitalism, built on the exploitation of labour, into images of a society far removed from the world of commodity production. As 'phantasmagorias', Wagner's operas embody the fundamental principles of mass culture (Adorno, 1981).

This is an interesting argument, which might be applied more plausibly to composers other than Wagner. The history of nineteenth-century opera, from Meyerbeer to Puccini, reflects the tendency for so-called high culture to accommodate itself to the demands of a burgeoning middle-class public, whose limited aesthetic tastes define art as entertainment and mindless spectacle. Applying this argument to the twentieth century, Adorno and Horkheimer went as far as to link the failure of socialism to the growth of a conformist mass culture, and saw in culture industry the means whereby modern industrial society (whether capitalist or state socialist) controls its population, not through force, but through culture. Culture industry maintains social order.

Thus the atomisation of modern society, in which the ideals of the Enlightenment – freedom, justice, autonomy of the individual – are eclipsed by mass conformity, has its cultural counterparts in the commodity nature of mass-produced art-forms. Adorno identifies the characteristic features of mass-produced art as repetition, 'endless recurrence' and 'pseudo-individuality' (mass art will share broadly similar themes, but it will be treated stylistically to produce a sense of something 'new', as individual and not created anonymously such as new forms of popular music). Leo Lowenthal described mass culture as 'psychoanalysis in reverse', because it produced repressed, unreflective and authoritarian personalities. Adorno echoes Lowenthal's analysis in his famous essay 'On the Fetishistic Character of Music and Regression of Hearing' (1938), in which he spelt out the effects of mass culture on the production and reception of art – 'vulgarisation', 'trivialisation', standardisation, a failure to communicate among a public increasingly 'moulded by anxiety, work and undemanding docility' (Adorno, 1991, p. 27).

Contemporary musical life, he concluded, was now 'dominated by the commodity form', with the 'ethereal and sublime' nature of music transformed into an aural background for modern advertising. In a world of mass consumption and the ubiquity of the commodity form, exchange value becomes the prime object of enjoyment. A visit to musical 'events' such as the Promenade Concerts in London or the first nights at the opera houses of La Scala and Covent Garden, is as much a social as an artistic occasion, a privileged access to an important cultural activity in which the pleasure conveyed through the ownership of a ticket frequently outweighs pleasure in the performance.

For Adorno, mass cultural norms effectively structure the field of classical music. It is not a question of mass culture constituting a separate realm from so-called high culture, because the whole of culture suffers from the dominance of the commodity form. Classical music is characterised by a 'fetishism' of standardised products (star conductors and soloists, a narrow range of concert and operatic repertory). And as individuals in the mass conform socially to conventional norms, this process finds its musical counterpart in the regression of hearing, a passive automatic listening in which musical elements are recognised momentarily only to be forgotten almost immediately. In the field of broadcasting classical music, the 'soundbite', a short aria or one movement from a concerto or symphony, reflects the growing tendency to adopt a pop music approach to musical culture. And, to further illustrate the relevance of Adorno's thesis, in 1996 the great conductor, Claudio Abbado, threatened to take Deutsche Grammophon to court for marketing, as a single record called *Adagio*, four of the Mahler adagios from his cycle of the symphonies.

In contemporary society, the musical soundbite is dominant: as Adorno noted, some fifty years before this term's invention, in mass society individuals listen atomistically. In a vein of deep pessimism, he writes that 'together with sport and film, mass music and the new listening help to make escape from the whole infantile milieu impossible' (Adorno, 1991, p. 41). Modern sport is a particular target for Adorno's animus, because it exemplifies, not the play element in culture, but rather 'a pseudo praxis' in which mass culture has successfully externalised as itself, an empty ritual, a passion which 'the masters of mass culture sense as the real basis... of power' (Adorno, 1989).

Culture, Class and Critique

Adorno's concept of culture functions at a number of different levels. Firstly, culture has its own distinctive sphere separate from the economic, political and social spheres: the promise of culture lies in its universal and affirmative essence, its repudiation of all utilitarian considerations ('the rationality of purpose') and its assumption of freedom: 'What is social about art is not its political stance, but its immanent dynamic in opposition to society... If any social function can be ascribed to art at all, it is the function to have no function' (Adorno, 1984, p. 322).

Secondly, this ideal, essentialist notion of culture contrasts starkly with the fundamentally utilitarian, purposive nature of modern mass culture. In this sense, all culture 'shares the guilt' of a society based on exploitation and injustice. In modern society mass cultural forms coexist with the more 'authentic modes'. Thus culture in all its variable forms must be analysed sociologically in terms of production, reproduction and reception. And, finally, although culture is necessarily embedded in a system of class inequality and class domination, it does not correspond in any significant way with class formation and class interests. The study of culture is weakened if undue emphasis is placed on such questions as the social background of artists and the search for relations of correspondence between class membership, social origin and the art work. Adorno's method is to focus on the internal structure of an art work, and by analysis reveal the social antagonisms 'sedimented' in aesthetic forms (Adorno, 1976, pp. 56–7).

Art represents society in complex ways. Music, for example, the most abstract of aesthetic forms, represents the 'life process' of society in the ways it expresses and interprets reality while simultaneously providing a critique of that same reality. Music represents society by transcending its immediate, empirical forms in its raising of questions about freedom and emancipation. Adorno identified Beethoven as one composer whose work expresssed the secular humanism and optimism of an emerging bourgeois class but whose music went beyond the narrow class interests and ideology of this class. To situate Beethoven sociologically it is necessary to analyse the changing social role of the artist: no longer dependent on religious and aristocratic patronage, composers such as Beethoven and Mozart were free to create music for a market and a new public, one open to the dynamic unfolding nature of music based in conflicting and sharply contrasting material. Beethoven sought to resolve all the inner tensions of his musical world by affirming the possibility of unity and wholeness, and celebrating the 'good society' by reconciling conflicts and differences within the ideal of an organic, unified artistic whole. Beethoven's music stands as a critique of a fragmented and alienated capitalist rationality.

Turning from production to reception, Adorno argues that Beethoven's music is gradually assimilated to an evolving bourgeois culture and a conservative public, for whom the composer is a 'classic', a reception which debases his 'pathos of humanity' into ritualistic celebrations of the *status quo*. For Adorno, this is the fate of all 'great music': created in opposition to the dictates of a market economy, music affirms its autonomy and commitment to emancipation of the subject, but musical production itself hinges on its relation to the market. And when the mechanisms of musical reproduction take over they transform music from 'critique' to 'entertainment' (Adorno, 1976, pp. 221–3). Music thus functions to form society through 'the more or less ritualised repetition of the mechanisms of integration employed by an already established social order'. On the one hand, music can rouse a critical sense of wholeness, generating a consciousness of society as an integrated totality and community: on the other, culture industry transforms great music into commodities available to a passive and atomised public (Adorno, 1973, p. 109).

The Problem of Method: Culture Industry and Cultural Memory

Unlike Marx and Gramsci, the Frankfurt School identify unity and coherence as the main constituents of capitalist culture, the theory of culture industry undermining the constituting role of social struggles and the pluralist nature of modern society. Morever, they assume direct links between culture and social order. There is, too, the problem of historical specificity. As Habermas observed, Adorno and Horkheimer assumed a globalising logic to capitalist development in that all industrial societies, whether capitalist or state socialist, were broadly similar in structure, an atomised mass and a highly centralised culture industry which eliminated all effective opposition and resistance. They saw little to choose between liberal, bourgeois democracy and fascist totalitarianism. The complex nature of modernity is thus assimilated to a one-dimensional concept of culture in which there is no room for active agents, only passive, ideologically indoctrinated masses.

This was the burden of Adorno's study of the astrology column of the *Los Angeles Times*, a content analysis of what he called institutionalised superstition. Horoscopes, he noted, feed a 'universal and alienated dependency', reinforcing the individual's sense of powerlessness and 'ego weakness', producing fatalistic and passive attitudes to life. There was no sense in Adorno's work that the readers of these columns might interpret the horoscopes in ways different from his own analysis. Adorno's research emphasised internal not external (reception) analysis, with individuals excluded from interpretative, even critical judgements: Adorno's reader is as much a 'cultural dope' as Parsons's actor, emptied of any potential reflexivity.

Cultural industry manipulates and controls art; consumerism and advertising coalesce, with standardised commodity production replacing critical and creative cultural expression:

> The assembly line character of the culture industry, the synthetic, planned method of turning out its products (factory-like not only in the studio but, more or less, in the compilation of cheap biographies, pseudo-documentary novels and hit songs) is very suited to advertising. The effect, the trick, the isolated repeatable device, have always been used to exhibit goods for advertising purposes... Advertising and the culture industry merge technically as well as economically. In both cases the same thing can be seen in innumerable places, and the mechanical repetition of the same cultural product has come to be the same as that of the propaganda slogan... the insistent demand for effectiveness makes technology into psychotechnology, into a procedure for manipulating men. (Adorno and Horkheimer, 1973, p. 163)

The Frankfurt School model of society is thus closed and finalised, a system which dominates from above, obeying the dehumanising logic of commodification and exploitation. Within this context the actual workings of reception are clearly problematic. The culture industry thesis assumes, for example, a strictly homologous relation between the art object and its public, that cultural consumers grasp and assimilate it in ways appropriate to its fixed, internal qualities. The argument that art has become a commodity does not necessarily suggest that it is experienced and interpreted as a commodity, or that commodified art-forms necessarily translate into commodified modes of reception. Much of contemporary rock music, for example, will resist incorporation into a dominant culture and, as with other forms of popular music, become increasingly marginalised within specific socio-cultural groups. It is not that such music develops novelty as 'pseudo-individuality' in opposition to the principles of standardisation at work in the market; rather, the originality of its form and language (especially with radical modes of rock music) militates against its mass appeal. To analyse all popular music as 'confirming' and reinforcing a 'psychological debasement', which violates human dignity and reduces aesthetic distance, is to ignore the living involvement, the imaginative grasp and creative use of popular music within distinct communities. The assumption that music should 'emancipate' the individual from an 'unfree society' is based on the false premise that culture affirms historical 'truth', that it somehow embodies and expresses transcendent universal values. But culture has no *telos* in this sense suggested by the Frankfurt School theory. With their common roots in Hegelian philosophy, both the Frankfurt School and Gramsci theorise culture as a historicist phenomenon which carries within it the marks of a potential utopia. Hence the false antinomy, so characteristic of Adorno's work, between high, affirmative culture and mass, popular culture.

However, this deeply pessimistic view which culture industry as a monolithic apparatus projects has been systematically undermined by recent research into the relations between audiences or readers and mass culture. One of the core assumptions of the culture industry thesis, that media texts express a single ideological meaning, has been challenged by a variety of empirical studies, which emphasise the polysemic nature of different texts, the coexistence of multiple meanings and possible interpretations. The concept of polysemic media opens the way for theorising the ways in which audiences and readers decode the structure of a cultural form. Research into television reception, for example, has frequently shown that interpretations of programmes, ranging from soap operas to documentaries, vary widely within the same social class. In his analysis of the popular television news-and-feature programme, *Nationwide*, Morley noted that the decoding of messages depended less on a shared economic and class position but more on 'the influences of the discourses and institution in which they are situated' (shop stewards, apprentices in factories, students, teachers in colleges of education; (Morley, 1980).

This is one of the main criticisms of the culture industry theory that the agent is constructed homogeneously by the cultural commodity, that she or he is inscribed as a subject within its ideological discourse. Thus, recalling Adorno's critique of astrology, Radway's research into the reading of romantic fiction suggests that rather than 'stitch the reader ever more resolutely into the fabric of patriarchical culture', reading the romance enables women to separate their domestic sphere from their pleasure sphere and derive from the act of reading 'often in explicit defiance of others' opposition...a new sense of strength and independence' (Radway, 1987, pp. 14–15). Although Adorno had noted in his article 'Culture Industry Reconsidered' (1957) the possibility of audience involvement in the construction of meanings (especially with television), this insight remained untheorised and unintegrated into the main body of the culture industry thesis (Adorno, 1991 pp. 85–92).

But this is not to deny the important contributions of both the Frankfurt School and Gramsci to the development of a Marxist theory of culture. Within both there exists a tension between the claims that history has an immanent meaning apart from its specific everyday forms, that the historical process expresses a narrative of practical freedom, and the open, fluid nature of culture itself with its basis in human practice. Hence the emphasis on culture industry as an organised system of domination, which seeks to destroy freedom and autonomy, the sense of continuity between one society and another, traditions and collective memory. If culture is the realm of memory, the storehouse of the past with its hopes, aspirations and practices which live actively within the present as new forms shaping the now-ness of today and the possibilities for the future, then culture industry constitutes the realm of non-culture, shattering the sense of the past, abolishing the historical sense and with it the concept of culture as the affirmation of freedom and the autonomy of the individual. Theorised during a period of nationally based media, culture industry is now more relevant than ever. In an era of global communications and profit-based cultural institutions dominated by massive capital invest-ment, the increasing decay of public service broadcasting and the trend towards homogenised media products and audiences, culture abandons 'otherness' and opposition to embrace the values of the market and mass society.

But what of the critical values that culture industry has flattened? As argued earlier, the Frankfurt School refuse to reduce the concept of culture to a way of life, but they offer no explanation for the genesis of those universal and transcendent values which generate affirmative culture and critical art. Who produces such values, under what social conditons and how do they become oppositional and utopian? What precisely are the mechanisms of production and reproduction? To draw on an antithesis between the reified, antihumanist values of culture industry and the authentic values of affirmative culture is to indulge in antihistorical abstractions and to empty culture of its specificity. In contrast, Gramsci's formulations point to a genetic, historical concept of culture in which the making and the remaking is deeply embedded in a living historical process. Culture involves struggles between dif-ferent social groups and classes within the framework of a pluralist civil society. For Gramsci, there was no total incorporation of the 'masses' into society as a whole; they are not rendered passive and incapable of criticism and critical practices. Moreover, Gramsci's emphasis on the historical roots of popular culture and the necessity to forge a national-popular culture through the concept of hegemony and social struggles involving active human agents constitutes a powerful corrective to Frankfurt School pessimism and determinism.

Chapter 4

Cultural Analysis and Systems Theory

The Concept of a Common Culture: From Durkheim to Parsons

As we have seen, the broad trend in the cultural sociology of Weber and Simmel lay in their attempts to theorise the developments of a specific domain of culture intrinsic to modernity. In Weber's case, culture was linked with social change, generating values which, once internalised by agents, led to the necessary motivations for particular modes of social action. For Weber, culture was bound up with the production and communication of meanings; it was an active, living process. As Clifford Geertz has noted, Weber conceives of man as 'an animal suspended in webs of significance he himself has spun', with culture consisting of those webs in which the analysis is 'not an experimental science in search of law but an interpretative one in search of meaning' (Geertz, 1973, p. 5). However, what should be added to Geertz's formulation is that Weber's cultural sociology goes beyond a narrowly focused semiotics, basing itself on broad historical transformations and, more particularly, on the pathologies of modernity.

In contrast to Weber's historical hermeneutics, Emile Durkheim's sociology, with its origins in the positivistic tradition of Comte and Taine, tended to underemphasise the communicative element in cultural analysis, especially Weber's focus on the problem of meaning, treating culture as an external objective social fact. But Durkheim's

53

significance for the sociology of culture lies in his attempts to go beyond sociological positivism (which was mainly the theoretical standpoint of his early work, notably *The Division of Labour in Society* and *Suicide*) and develop what Jeffrey Alexander has called 'a cultural logic for society', to theorise culture not simply as an external structure but rather as a relatively autonomous process of beliefs and human practices (Alexander, 1990). Thus in his study *The Elementary Forms of the Religious Life* (1915) Durkheim examined the role played by 'collective representations' in social life seeking to link ritual and symbolic forms with problems of social integration and social solidarity.

In his early work Durkheim had adopted a modified base–superstructure model in order to distinguish between the material basis of society (which included the volume and density of the population, territorial organisation and levels of technological development) and its institutional structure (consisting of the religious, educational and family institutions). This latter normative sphere involved both beliefs and practices, as well as collective representations, collective forms of action bound up with moral concepts, legal rules and religious notions (embodied in ideologies such as nationalism, socialism, religion, etc.). Durkheim argued that in conditions where the material structure was dominant the individual was wholly constrained, lacking any real autonomy; in contrast, if the institutional, normative sphere is relatively independent then the individual has greater freedom and choice. As society evolves from pre-modern to modern forms of social solidarity, the institutional – normative sphere becomes more and more autonomous. For Durkheim, social solidarity was possible only if the normative embodied moral and universal values, elements which individuals accept and internalise as desirable ends in themselves and not as relativist values linked with individual and group interests.

It would be wrong, then, to reduce Durkheim's cultural theory to a form of positivism. Culture is not defined, or theorised, in terms of external, reified and constraining structures, but as a symbolic order, a universe of shared meanings which effectively motivate individuals through values and ideas. Culture is thus defined as a pattern of meanings embodied in symbolic forms (collective representations) which exist both in and outside the individual. It is through these collective structures that individuals share experiences, concepts and beliefs and effectively communicate with each other. In this way social solidarity is not something externally imposed but a process achieved symbolically through mediated intersubjective action. Culture is, therefore, a way of life in which the existence of common values secures the normative consensus necessary for social order.

Durkheim emphasised that symbolic forms existing independently of individuals constitute structures which cannot be reduced to social interaction (Simmel's position). Implicit here is the argument that within society there exists a common culture based on shared experiences and values, in which symbolic forms function to maintain social solidarity. Thus the role played by the 'sacred' in religion, in collective experience and action, as a realm separate from the mundane and utilitarian world of everyday life expresses universal and therefore binding values. Individuals internalise values as moral imperatives, acting not merely for their own individual interests but universally for all members of the collectivity.

Durkheim's cultural theory suggests that it is the symbolic order which functions to generate the values necessary for social unity. Social life 'in all its aspects and in every period of its history, is made possible only by a vast symbolism' (Durkheim, 1957, p. 231). Hence the soldier who dies for his country dies for the flag and this is the symbol which has priority in his consciousness. Although a sign with no value in itself, the flag represents reality and is treated as if it was reality. Symbolic forms thus constitute their own reality, and in his analysis of Australian totemism Durkheim notes how the totem functioned to unite individuals, who were dispersed into small hordes, into a single moral community:

> Now the totem is the flag of the clan. It is, therefore, natural that the impressions aroused by the clan in individual minds...should fix themselves to the idea of the totem rather than that of the clan: for the clan is too complex a reality to be represented clearly in all its complex unity by such rudimentary intelligences. More than that, the primitive does not even see that these impressions come to him from the group. He does not know that the coming together of a number of men associated in the same life results in disengaging new energies, which transform each of them. All that he knows is that he is raised above himself and that he sees a different life from the one he ordinarily leads. (ibid., p. 220)

A heightened sense of social solidarity is produced by the effervescence generated by great collective gatherings and the symbolic representations employed. The collective ceremonies represent the past, 'fixing it firmly in the mind' and awakening 'certain ideas and sentiments, to attach the present to the past or the individual to the group' (ibid., pp. 376–8). Similar collective sentiments characterise modern culture: the French Revolution transformed the ideas of liberty and reason into sacred things to erect around them a secular religion with its dogmas, symbols, altars and feasts. For Durkheim, then, such festivals function to renew social order and tradition by forging a sense of social continuity and feelings of solidarity as the individual is integrated with the collectivity.

But in opposing the crude Marxist reductionism of culture to material forces (a common theme of French Marxists of Durkheim's generation), Durkheim offered a new reductionism: culture as a functional imperative for social unity and social integration responsive to the needs of the collectivity. In this sense, Durkheim's cultural theory has a tendency to elide the cultural and the social. However, his emphasis on the importance of collective memory and on ways in which collective representation links individuals, not simply to a social group but to the past, is of crucial significance. But Durkheim's functionalist methodology succeeds in transforming the concept of memory from a potentially dynamic historical category into a static, closed and ahistorical notion. By defining the symbolic order in terms of an ideally integrated society, Durkheim strips culture of its 'otherness', its negative and critical potential in which memory actively distils from the past what is alive and significant for the present, for the hopes and aspirations of social groups as they seek meaning and purpose for their lives.

Common Culture: Parsons

Durkheim's notion of transcendent values and his concept of culture as symbolically mediated interaction becomes further developed in the early work of Talcott Parsons, notably his *The Structure of Social Action* (1937), which seeks a grand synthesis of the classical sociological tradition of Durkheim and Weber. Parsons proposed what he called a voluntaristic theory of action, in which the principle of action was closely linked with the internalisation of cultural values and an emphasis on the action element in the construction of social order. The question of social integration was resolved by focusing on a core of common values and norms accepted as legitimate by social agents. In his later work, however, notably *The Social System* (1951), Parsons's action approach increasingly became subsumed by systems theory, a standpoint which had the effect of diminishing the voluntaristic element in favour of macro-structural-functionalist models. Whereas in *The Structure of Social Action* Parsons's starting point had been the 'unit act', in his later structural-functionalist works the starting point was that of 'the empirical system' and macro social structure, with the focus shifting to 'the integration of the motivation of actors with the normative cultural standards which integrate the action system' (Parsons, 1951).

In this later, explicitly functionalist phase, Parsons emphasised the critical role played by culture in social systems theory. Writing of Marx, Parsons described historical materialism as 'psychologically naïve' for its failure to account for the significance of cultural factors in the maintenance of social order, social integration and equilibrium. Underlying the normative structure are specific 'cultural codes', which provide 'directionality of orientations to work and enterprise' (Parsons, 1967, pp. 123–35). In this formulation, Parsons redefines his concept of culture from that of his early voluntaristic theory: culture is no longer linked with the autonomy principle but embedded in and reduced to the social system level, a standpoint at variance with the cultural sociology of Weber and Simmel. In Parsons's tortuous formulation, culture is defined now as 'patterned' or ordered systems of symbols (the object of the orientation of actions), internalised components of the personalities of individual actors and institutionalised patterns of the social system (Parsons, 1951, p. 327). Indeed, the thrust of Parsons's account of culture lies in its emphasis on the mechanisms whereby values become successfully internalised. In this way culture itself constitutes 'the generalised aspect of the organisation of action systems' (Parsons, 1955, p. 31). Cultural elements mediate and regulate the communicative and interaction process (Parsons, 1951, p. 32).

To be sure, Parsons attempts to distinguish between social and cultural institutions by theorising culture as a distinctive sphere, or system. He argues that a common value system constitutes an essential prerequisite for social integration. And the highest normative components are cultural values, not social system values from which they must be clearly distinguished. Thus culture as symbolically meaningful systems (patterns of ideas, values) shapes both human behaviour and the resulting artefacts. In contrast, society, or the social system, relates to 'the specifically relational system of interaction among the individual and collectivities' (Kroeber and Parsons, cited Bourricard, 1981, p. 174). Society, therefore, does not reflect cultural values, nor does culture reflect social relations, the patterns of social interaction. This is one of Parsons's major theoretical insights, that although culture provides for those 'ultimate meanings' which he argues are inseparable from motivation, culture at no point is reducible to motivation or to social interaction. However, the emphasis on normative consensus as the basis of social order leads Parsons to elide the distinction between, and the autonomy of, the cultural and the social: he writes, for example, of the normative order constituting the structure of the self, and of social actors as reflexes of the social system. At the same time, he holds firmly to the theory of a central value system, a common culture which functions as a normatively integrating structure.

Parsons had rejected positivistic theories of voluntarism for their assumption that all forms of human action were reducible to the contextual conditions of action: his point was that cultural values, because of their close link with social integration, necessarily enshrine universal values, and not everyday, context-bound and thus relativist ones. If cultural values are to make an effective contribution to the social cohesion of society as a whole then they must be universal:

> Values are the principles from which less general norms and expectations can be derived. They stand on a level of generality which is independent of any specific situational object-structure, external to the social system of reference or internal to it. (Parsons, 1989, p. 579)

Parsons stressed the necessity to define values 'as independent of any specific level of structural differentiation of the system in which they are held'. Through participation in the common culture of society, the individual defines what is desirable and valuable. Cultural values become simultaneously institutionalised in the subsystems of society and internalised by individuals, differentiated into ideas, norms, judgements and values. In this way 'the higher normative components of culture' enable individuals to transcend their particular embodiment in social institutions, their meaning realised through action which goes beyond empirical everyday experience (ibid., pp. 577–82).

Parsons's main point, therefore, is the existence of a unified value system which functions in ways which maintain social integration. To be sure, he stresses that no social system is perfectly integrated and that there will always be imbalances between the cultural and the social system: only a utopian would project a perfectly equilibrated, integrated society, although the value system of modern society necessarily strives to this ideal. Where further developments in structural differentiation occur this does not alter the fundamental value system: although changes take place in the subsystems, Parsons concludes by proposing a fundamental stability to American values stretching across great tracts of historical time and variable social and political structures. American values have hardly changed in their universality from the earliest colonial period to the modern present: a stable party system with strong liberal values, equality of opportunity based on strongly held values of individualism, and a pluralism which militates against both weak and 'overtight' integration.

Although Parsons's theorisation of culture emphasises the critical principle of autonomy, his empirical analysis suggests the opposite, that culture is closely tied in with the dominant ideological values of an emerging and triumphant capitalism. More particularly, his approach is anti-genetic: how are cultural values produced, who is responsible for their development and integration into society? To what extent are cultural values divisive, generating conflict and struggle between different social groups? Parsons's sociology is equally ambivalent on the problem of the reproduction of cultural values, and his work appears to be close to a sociological version of the dominant ideology thesis. However, his basic argument that values are transferred from culture to the social system non-mechanically and non-problematically assumes that cultural values are not identical with their context, possessing universal and transcendent qualities. Cultural values are non-finite, and Parsons's position is Durkheimian in its basic proposition that the integration of social systems depends on universally binding values which cut across pragmatic and interest-based values. In this sense, Parsons is closer to Gramsci than to the Frankfurt School. However, Parsons's theoretical standpoint, while of great interest for the sociology of culture, is ultimately weakened both by the narrowly conceived concept of a common culture (as a closed and finalised structure) and by the failure to address the problem of conflict over cultural values and the coexistence of alternatives within the same social context.

To argue for a stable and common culture in a society riven with racial divisions and conflict, together with the persistence of widespread racial discrimination against Afro-Americans, effectively assimilates and marginalises different cultural values to a 'higher' level. Parsons's model fails to raise one of the critical issues of a cultural sociology, the possibility that cultural values may work to exclude specific social groups from the broad social structure, rather than include them in it. Moreover, the meaning and significance of cultural values will be interpreted differently by social groups as they seek to impose their definitions on others. In effect, Parsons exaggerates the degree of coherence of culture and society, advancing an idealist concept of high levels of coherence between cultural values and the cultural system.

There is, too, the problem of teleology. Parsons's work suggests that in the production of culture the agent realises already existing values rather than being actively involved in their creation. Culture functions behind the backs of agents. And it has a hidden 'purpose' in generating the basis for social integration. But the link between the agent and the system remains deeply problematic. In arguing that in the act of realising universal cultural values the bonds between the individual and the normative culture are deepened, Parsons is open to the criticism of ethnomethodologists such as Harold Garfinkel, that the agent is merely a 'cultural dope' whose actions comply with 'standardised expectations' and 'who produce[s] the stable features of society by acting in compliance with pre-established and legitimate alternatives...that the common culture provides' (Garfinkel, 1967, pp. 66–8).

Parsons's cultural sociology thus assumes a neatly ordered social world, closed and finalised, in which a diverse range of social groups are successfully incorporated, while others, failing to assimilate universal normative culture, are excluded from the process of cultural unity. As Margaret Archer has suggested, Parsons has defined culture so that all possible contradictions are eliminated, and this theory fails to deal with structural differentiation as a possible basis of conflictual power relations (Archer, 1989, p. 34). In effect, Parsons offers a reworking of the 'myth of cultural integration', a focus on consistent, coherent cultural patterns derived from social system values which then function to shape all other actions. There is no explanation for the domination of specific cultural values, and Parsons's theory offers no mechanism which might account for their historical genesis. Nor does the theory account for conflict over cultural values or conflict within culture itself.

Unlike Gramsci, Parsons analyses the 'universal' transcending elements of culture (which involve an important distinction between cultural and ideological values) in a way which eliminates the 'making' and the corresponding 'linkages' involved between social groups and their position within hierarchies of power and status. Parsons separates values from ideology by arguing that the latter functions at a lower level of generality than values dealing with the 'existential' state of the world. In contrast, 'the primary reference for considering the cultural integration of a social system is the degree of commonness or sharedness of its values in all parts of its structure e.g. "classes" of its population' (Parsons, 1989, p. 580). But because active agents play no real role in this process the result is a teleological account of cultural change and cultural stability. The fundamental weakness of both Parsons's and Durkheim's cultural sociologies lies here, in a failure to deal with questions of doing, the human and the institutional modes of producing and reproducing culture and values in societies characterised by unequal access to the major cultural institutions. The positing of universal values is analytically unhelpful, because without a concept of an active agent whose practices help to shape the social world, cultural change must inevitably flow out of those depersonalising forces linked to the central value system which 'orchestrate sociocultural integration'. Such a standpoint has the effect of transforming the past into an inert and dead process emptied of those 'signs and evidences... of creative resources which can sustain the present and prefigure possibility' (Thompson, 1981, pp. 407–8).

Parsons's sociology effectively closes off this avenue by its concentration on an idealised, essentialist concept of cultural values. The relation between culture in this sense and culture in the everyday world is unclear. Unlike Gramsci, Parsons has no conception of the organic links between popular culture and universal culture, of the ways in which individuals, through their everyday practices (which often involve creative, imaginative thinking and recourse to stocks of knowledge) produce and reproduce cultural values as responses to their social world, and as the means of understanding and mastering it, thus producing the basis for elements of universality.

Habermas: Culture and Communicative Practice

Parsons's sociology shares with Western Marxism (notably the Frankfurt School and Gramsci) the foregrounding of culture as a significant element in the sociological analysis of modern industrial society. His fundamental disagreement with Marxism lay in the argument that Marx had failed to account for the process whereby values became internalised by agents and thus had concentrated excessively on capitalism as an economic system. Marx and Marxism were of limited value for those sociologists concerned with the important role played by ideas and values in culture, in the shaping of social order and the interaction between ideas and social change. But the fundamental weakness of Parsons's work on culture and its role in the social system lay in its failure to theorise the concept of culture as a 'making of values' through the actions of collective agents.

Broadly similar criticisms can be levelled at the Frankfurt School's concepts of culture industry, one-dimensional man, and the modern capitalism as dominated by a dehumanised rationality. Nevertheless, unlike Parsonian functionalism, the Frankfurt School's theory of modern culture has exerted and continues to exert an enormous influence on the social and cultural sciences. It appears to many theorists to offer a more salient analysis of modern society than either the dogmatic prescriptions of Leninist Marxism or the rigid formulations of structural functionalism. But as Habermas has observed, the Frankfurt School programme, initiated by Max Horkheimer and Adorno, effectively ignored the historically complex and variable practices of the everyday social world, reducing them to mere ideological reflexes of a centralised culture industry. The central propositions advanced by the critical theorists hinged on a highly speculative philosophy of history, which tended to marginalise specific empirical and historical analysis of the relations between the forces and relations of production. The goal of capitalist rationality was the total domination of society through administration and instrumental values. Thus the tendency of the Frankfurt School theorists was to conceive capitalism as a single universal system and, by extension, to argue that its basic features were further mirrored in the closed, administered, totalitarian systems of communism and fascism. All modern industrial societies followed a similar logic based in a highly centralised state apparatus and a passive, atomised mass. As an integral part of the capitalist mode of production, culture industry brought unity to the political, economic and cultural levels; within, there existed no real differentiation of structure and ideology. The result was a static, one-dimensional concept of society in which all significant social change either had been abolished or was simply absent. An atomised social structure was paralleled by a homogeneous ruling stratum and dominant ideology in which all social struggles ceased as constituting processes; and all opposition both internally and externally had been abolished.

As the leading figure of the second generation of critical theorists, Jurgen Habermas has consistently sought to develop a sociology of modern society which avoids the bleak pessimism of Adorno and Horkheimer and the teleological basis of the Frankfurt School theory. He argues for a radical revision of Marxism in the direction of an adequate concept of culture: in place of the dominant culture thesis, culture must be theorised in terms of action and communication. For Habermas, the basic elements of historical materialism – notably the base–superstructure model – must be extended by introducing the notion of humanity as both a toolmaking and speaking agent: the theory of communicative action shifts the focus from economic production to linguistically mediated social interaction, thus bringing to the fore the process of social reproduction. He criticises the tendency of some Marxists to 'reduce' society to a single dimension of collective social labour (Marx's 'productivist model') in which language is defined as a mere reflex rather than as an autonomous structure deeply involved in social and cultural development: 'From Hegel through Freud to Piaget the idea has developed that subject and object are reciprocally constituted, the subject can grasp hold of itself only in relation to and by way of the construction of an objective world' (Habermas, 1979, pp. 98–100). In this way Habermas conceives social systems as constituting 'networks of communicative actions' involving socialised personalities and speaking subjects.

Habermas's second departure from the basic tenets of critical theory lies in his distinction between society as a 'system', and society as a 'life-world', or the everyday world of culture, personality, meanings and symbols, to the economic and political imperatives of a centralised and rationalised system. In sharp contrast with the first generation of critical theorists, Habermas argues that the concept of society must be theorised simultaneously as both system and life-world. It is through the life-world and its institutions and variable practices that communication becomes possible as agents seek mutual understanding through speech and action. In Adorno's and Horkheimer's formulations, everyday life was saturated with ideological and reified structures, the manifestations of a dominant authoritarian state. Habermas thus sets himself against this closed and pessimistic model.

Habermas defines the life-world as a differentiated structure closely bound up with cultural values and communicative practices. When individuals seek to communicate with each other, the life-world constitutes the context of verbal and social interaction. The life-world, so to speak, stands behind the backs of the participants, characterised by implicit assumptions about traditions and values. Communication takes place through the hidden structures of the life-world. In contrast, the system works through the overt mechanism of production, money, power, through the institutions of the economy and the state. It is thus the case that within the system and its various subsystems, action is 'instrumental', with goals narrowly defined in terms of existing institutions. These system imperatives contribute functionally to the maintenance of the social system as a whole.

The relationship between system and life-world is not, however, as straightforward as Habermas's revision of critical theory might suggest. He argues against Adorno and Horkheimer that life-world and system constitute separate dimensions of society as a whole, and that in the course of modernity the life-world increasingly becomes independent of system imperatives. In pre-industrial society, culture and personality were wholly imbricated in the economic and political structures (for example, Habermas cites the case of primitive society, where kinship structures were mostly inseparable from the units of production; in modern society the economic institutions of production have become increasingly differentiated from those of kinship). In pre-industrial society it was impossible to differentiate life-world and system; with the coming of industrialism the emphasis falls on the autonomy of the life-world and its internal differentiation. Cultural reproduction works through the life-world securing both 'a continuity of tradition and coherence of knowledge sufficient for daily practice'.

Habermas's standpoint is the opposite of the mass culture thesis: the coexistence of differing communicative practices within the life-world suggests the possibility for open, free discourse among active not passive agents. To be sure, culture in the strict Frankfurt School sense of a highly organised, concentrated structure built around homogeneity of products and profits remains. But culture industry, as a totally dominating presence which absorbs all alternative modes of communication, is rejected as an ahistorical abstraction. Habermas notes that within the sphere of the life-world new social and cultural movements may emerge with values at odds with those of dominant 'formal' system imperatives linked to economic production, power and money. He cites social movements such as the Greens and Women's Liberation as exemplifying this move to the 'substantive' values associated with the quality of life, emancipation and communicative action.

Habermas is thus arguing that the differentiation of the life-world – the spheres of art, science, politics, ethics – generates those principles of autonomy which enable agents to live a more 'rational' life and communicate through free and equal discourse. The Frankfurt School ideal, the 'project of Enlightenment', clearly remains a possibility: individuals possess the capacity for self-reflection, understanding and knowledge. By basing his theory on a model of communication and not production, Habermas is able to posit an ideal state of 'undistorted communication' as the ultimate goal of the life-world, the conversation of free citizens in which 'truth' emerges through a process of open dialogue. The life-world is autonomous, thus enabling a rational communicative action to take place, a linguistically mediated interaction based on the principles of cooperation not those of force and coercion, on dialogue which seeks to establish a normative consensus. All this opens the way for genuine human emancipation.

However, the dark side of this picture lies in the permanent tension between life-world and system, which remains especially acute in contemporary society. System imperatives governing production and profitability, the steering media of money and power combined with an increasing role for the state, seek to penetrate the structures of the life-world, thus distorting linguistically mediated interaction and undermining the rational and universal elements of truth embedded in language. Language itself now becomes dominated by the functional imperatives of formal, instrumental rationality, distorted communication which is imbricated with domination. If system imperatives succeed in 'colonising' the life-world in this way the result will be a centralisation of culture, bureaucratic rationality, increasing passivity and the decline of autonomy.

Habermas's theory of culture clearly owes much to the critical theory of the Frankfurt School and the systems theory of Parsons. Both emphasise the *telos* of culture, its universal, transcendent elements. Habermas, however, distinguishes between Marx's stress on social labour as the foundation of society and his own model of communication, in which language forms the basis of social and cultural development. Adopting a communication rather than a productivist model of society, however, has the effect of separating the 'making' of language, the wide variety of its usages (in actual speech) and the institutions which enable language use to develop. Habermas's emphasis on communication further downgrades living, everyday speech in favour of ideal, universalising language. But communication (intersubjective interaction) occurs through the different modes of using language at different levels of society, a process closely bound up with labour. Language exists through labour, produced in situations which enable individuals to situate themselves in the social world and establish relations with others. Everyday speech and communication (Gramsci's popular culture) forms the basis of more complex modes of interaction, but Habermas reverses this relationship by situating the principle of open dialogue within an ideal sphere of rational practices carried out by knowledgeable agents. However, this is to marginalise the role of individual and collective agents in the genesis of dialogue and communication; the result is a theorisation of cultural development as the product of impersonal system imperatives which pose dangers to the existence of culture itself.

Similar criticisms can be levelled at the theory of rationalisation as a world-historical process which Habermas proposes as the explanation of the rapid development and revolutionising of the forces of production with the resultant uncoupling of the economic and political systems from the cultural system. For while Habermas links Weber's principle of autonomy historically with the rise of civil society and the bourgeois public sphere (cultural institutions separate from the state and independent of market forces, which enabled the bourgeois class to participate in open, democratic discussion and dialogue with others), his theory of the colonisation of the life-world (of which the public sphere constituted a structural and integral element) suggests both a pessimistic and deterministic standpoint at odds with his rejection of the Frankfurt School theory. The problem is that Habermas has assimilated the making of these processes, and particularly the collective labour which underpins them, to an underlying, ahistorical logic. Paradoxically, Habermas claims his approach as a form of genetic structuralism, but it lacks any real sense of historical time and specificity. The concepts of undistorted communication, life-world and system tend to lifeless abstractions analytically weak for grasping the complex and variable structures of contemporary society, the variety of cultural institutions and practices, and establishing the degree and nature of their autonomy. As with critical theory, Habermas fails to ground Weber's thesis of cultural differentiation contextually and to specify the internal complexity and hierarchical structure of the different spheres.

Habermas has argued that in positing a tension between the life-world and system, and between system and social integration, his model achieves the dynamism missing from Parsonian functionalism. But like Parsons, he fails to develop an adequate sociological concept of agency and to raise questions of the making of structures: communicative rationality, the life-world and system are theorised in functionalist terms, stripped of any real historical dynamism, conceived as abstractly dehumanised processes working behind and not through agents and their variable everyday practices. In short, in both Habermas and Parsons a notion of social interaction between agents at different levels of society, which both generates cultural values and acts as the medium for their further development, is missing. Culture is instantiated in patterns of social interaction, given its living everyday forms. But both sociological and Marxist functionalism collapse culture into system needs and imperatives and separate function from human action.

Culture and Interaction

One of the fundamental weaknesses of systems theory lies in its failure to theorise both the making of culture and its relation with everyday practices and institutions. In contrast, sociological interactionism (the microsociology associated with Mead, Garfinkel and Goffman) by focusing on microcontexts (such as the cultural and social life of jazz musicians and working-class subcultures) has attempted to avoid the reification implicit in functionalism by arguing that both culture and the social self arise directly out of a process of sociation. Goffman, for example, taking up some of the concepts associated with Simmel, has developed an empirically based sociology of cultural forms and symbolic orders in which he explores the ways in which individuals strive to retain their sense of identity and self through developing particular strategies within the interaction process. Everyday interaction provides the basis for the construction of meaning, and Goffmann's work examines the most ordinary and banal moments of everyday life as the basis of cultural value.

In his important essay 'The Interaction Order' (1983), Goffman argued that face-to-face interaction constituted a *sui generis* order characterised by its own distinctive properties and boundaries, a structure irreducible to the macroinstitutional order. Its properties, such as language, symbols, knowledge, etc., enable agents to participate in various forms of action and, at the same time, commit themselves to the underlying coherence and 'orderliness' of the order itself. In his studies of total institution, *Asylums* (1961), Goffman noted the tendency for institutions such as prisons, asylums and mental hospitals to generate a depersonalised social order, to strip the individual of identity, to restructure and recategorise it: but within these institutions there develops an interaction order separate from the larger institutional forms, its moral and cultural resources providing the basis for individuals to preserve both their sense of identity and their responsibility.

But how is this interaction order linked with the macro order? In his studies of language, *Forms of Talk* (1981) especially, Goffman seems to suggest that society exists and is integrated loosely through talk, with everyday conversation acting as a ritual affirmation of a common shared reality: talk has a key symbolic role in defining, strengthening and maintaining the structure of social groups and patterns of interaction. Talk creates a world of other participants, in which conversation 'has a life of its own and makes demands on its own behalf... a little social system with its own boundary maintaining tendencies' (Goffman, 1972, p. 113). Goffman's point is that as the self arises out of this process it is constituted at the macro level by symbolic forms based on ritual, shared meanings and culture. Hence the politeness in everyday interaction is comparable to religious ceremonies with their notion of the human personality as a sacred object and moral value inherent in communion (conversation, interaction) with others (ibid., pp. 73, 95). Thus the institutional and interaction orders are 'loosely coupled', sharing in broadly similar symbolic forms.

While Goffman's 'loose coupling' of the micro and macro orders represents an important corrective to systems theory, it does not address the critical problem of the hierarchical nature of interaction itself. Culture exists and plays an active role at both the micro level and the macro; within both everyday social life and large-scale institutions there is interaction structured in terms of positions which agents occupy. But Goffman's separation of these two orders severs the very real empirical links between them and projects a narrowly conceived concept of contextualisation. It is important for a cultural sociology to develop a concept of active agent involved in distinctive patterns of social interaction, to identify the properties whereby agents relate to the social world and evolve different forms of action, to grasp that agents are knowledgeable, imaginative and reflexive. A more rigorous mode of sociological and historical contextualisation (both synchronic and diachronic) is required than is possible within both Goffman's narrowly conceived interaction order and the abstract systems approach of Parsons and Habermas. The following two chapters take up these problems of agency, context and hierarchy.

Chapter 5

Contextualising Culture

Context and Culture

I have argued in previous chapters that the theorisation of culture in sociology focused primarily on culture's role in social change, socialisation and everyday life; Marxist theorists went further, attempting to develop a cultural theory based in aesthetic problems seeking to elucidate the links between culture and different forms of art and literature. A major preoccupation shared by Marxists (notably Gramsci) and sociologists (especially Weber, Simmel and Parsons) was the growing autonomy of culture and the necessity to develop analytical concepts to address this issue. However, this emphasis on the principle of autonomy, while challenging reductionist accounts of culture and the non-problematic assimilation to specific elements in the social structure, never succeeded in adequately integrating the 'ideal' with the social–material determinants of cultural forms and production. Culture became synomous with essentialist universal values, floating free of its social context. Thus Parsons, following Kant, identified a transcendent core of values, hopes and aspirations which, embedded in specific socio-historical contexts, form an autonomous cultural realm above material social life.

The autonomisation of culture constitutes one of the central themes of both classical sociology and the Marxism of Gramsci and the Frankfurt School. However, the problem of tracing the links between the autonomy of culture and its basis in a social context, potentially a highly complex methodological issue, was at best theorised ambiguously and philosophically, or assimilated to a homogenising notion of culture industry or the central value system. Similarly, Simmel's meta-narrative of the tragedy of culture severed all empirical and historical links between culture and society and eliminated all concepts of an active human agent.

Missing from these analyses is the historical sense, that the culture of the present has been made and fashioned to give meaning to individual lives through time and within distinct social groups. A major problem for the sociology of culture lies in theorising the precise relations between different social groups, or fractions of groups, and the production and reproduction of culture. All societies are structured in hierarchical relations and unequal access to different forms of culture and power. This principle of hierarchical structure, with its clear implications for the processes of cultural production and reproduction (and consumption or reception) has rarely been integrated analytically into cultural theory. Who produces culture? What kind of culture? And what precisely are the links between different producers and the variable cultural traditions and formations of any society? Such questions raise problems of the exact mechanisms governing production and reproduction, and of the nature of the linkages between the micro level of social groups and the macro level of society as a whole. To theorise culture sociologically it is essential to analyse both its external and internal components, the variety of cultural practices involving active human agents (both individual and collective) which produce specific forms of culture with their own distinctive properties. Situating culture contextually involves a dialectical process of constantly shifting from the external to the internal while grounding the analysis in a structured notion of socio-cultural context, one which takes account of internal differentiation and hierarchical levels.

Of course, social contexts do not present themselves as flat terrains but as complex formations with specific internal structures. A failure to specify the structural differentiation of socio-cultural context is characteristic of both evolutionary and functionalist theories of culture, which, as Margaret Archer has noted, assume patterns of harmony and coherence between interdependent parts, with the function of culture identified as the production of social order through 'stable' normative elements (Archer, 1989). Such theories fail to advance a specific method for analysing and theorising culture in its historical forms and social contexts. In contrast, while Simmel and the Frankfurt School theorists break from functionalist and evolutionary theory, they theorise culture in essentialist and philosophical terms, failing to contextualise sociologically. The weakness of these theories is a failure to generate specific analytical concepts which provide the tools for empirical investigation of the social and historical context of cultural production. Forexample, social contexts exist in space and time, but in the work of Simmel, Durkheim and Parsons contexts are only loosely located through time and space. In place of specific contexts, which pass through historical time, many Marxist and socio-logical theories advance transcultural generalisations which focus on so-called 'laws' and 'tendencies', on macrostructures such as society conceived as a 'totality' or as an integrated system.

Contextualising Music: The Problem of Mediation

Adorno highlights many of these issues in his studies in the sociology of literature, art and music, in which the method of searching for patterns of correspondence between the social origins of artists and their art forms is superseded by the Hegelian notion of mediation through the social whole. The relation of aesthetic content to social context is dialectical, not functional. In his studies of music, for example, he raises the problem of how external social forces (the social context) enter and shape the formal internal properties of the musical structure. Adorno's solution was to argue that music repres-ents, indirectly, almost unconsciously, the 'life-process' of society, expressing, interpreting and critiquing reality. It is the inner structure of musical composition which provides the answer to the problematic relation of music to society. For musical forms internalise the social antinomies, so that music's language 'sketches' the contradictions and imperfections of existing society. Social contradictions are 'sedimen-ted' in musical forms: music thus expresses opposition to and the necessity to overcome such tensions. Music confirms 'the emancipa-tion of the subject' through its own internal dynamics, its rejection of simplified modes of communication and its refusal to accommodate itself to the principles of the market-place. The 'fissures' and 'frac-tures' within musical form embody the 'promise of culture', of free-dom, the striving for utopia. As examples, Adorno cites Bach and his 'pathos of humanity', which is deeply inscribed in his music, and Beethoven, whose music enjoys strong affinities with bourgeois libertarianism to constitute 'a dynamically unfolding totality'. In

Beethoven's symphonies and string quartets the separate movements develop, negate, confirming both themselves 'and the whole without looking outward', thus resembling 'the world whose forces move them' but not 'by imitating that world' (Adorno, 1976, pp. 68–70, 209). The category of the social is thus represented in music not through identifying a particular ideology or world view of a social class or group (to which the composer may belong) but in the ways the musical material itself expresses society as a whole. The dynamic tensions at work within the musical material of classical music, especially Beethoven, constitute social problems (and thus the social context transmuted into abstract and non-conceptual language). Thus Beethoven's celebration of human emancipation finds expression in the 'affirmative gestures' of the symphonic reprises, which assume 'the force of crushing repression, of an authoritative "That's how it is"... the cryptogram for the senselessness of a merely self-reproducing reality that has been welded together into a system' (ibid., p. 210). Later classical composers (notably Rossini, Berlioz, Wagner and Stravinsky) adapted pragmatically to the capitalist consumer market, producing music more 'partial', less autonomous, 'atrophying' and incapable of presenting society 'as a dynamic totality' but rather 'as a series of pictures' (ibid., p. 69, 211; Adorno, 1973, p. 29).

However, the problem of context is not so easily resolved by recourse to the categories of totality and mediation. Adorno tends to employ the concept of totality in two distinct ways: first, as an integral element in an empirical methodology which facilitates research into the relations between the immanent properties of art and its socio-cultural historical context; and second, as a philosophical historicist category linked to a metanarrative with utopia as its *telos*. It is this latter notion which enables Adorno to differentiate 'progressive' art from 'reactionary' forms, art which refuses to accept consumerist culture (for example the atonal music of Schoenberg) from art which bends its knee to capitalist rationality (the neo-classical music of Stravinsky). But as Martin Jay has pointed out, Adorno's fundamental methodological principle is that 'only a theoretically informed investigation of the mediated social relations *within* the cultural artefact itself can illuminate its full significance' (Jay, 1984, p. 118, his emphasis). However, the social relations that constitute the structure of the social context must also be theorised, grasped in their hierarchically organised forms which remain irreducible to any one dominant element such as the economic. The hierarchical levels of social contexts, equally, possess the potential for varying degrees of autonomy. The weakness of Adorno's anti-reductionist notion of context is that it tends to flatten and smooth out all the contradictory elements and levels, effectively reducing the notion of context to an addendum of internal aesthetic structure. He notes, for example, that works of art necessarily depend on society, on a specific mode of production and concomitant social structure, although simultaneously existing within their own autonomous sphere. But his formulations, however, have the effect of isolating and severing the cultural process from the active, shaping forces of everyday social interaction. The art work is social in its active relations with social context, which comprises patterns of interaction at both the everyday level and the institutional. To theorise the problem of contextualisation in terms of a suprahistorical concept of totality eliminates both the process of making the context (through collective social labour and action) and the making of culture and art. Adorno's theorisation of culture and context closes off empirical investigation, foregrounding a deeply non-problematic notion of context.

Cultural Materialism

As I have argued, the work of Gramsci and the Frankfurt School represented a significant turn towards the development of cultural Marxism from within Marxism itself, an anti-positivism which aimed to re-evaluate the base–superstructure model throughout the concepts of totality, mediation, praxis and the materiality of culture. In this way the dualisms inherent in positivism would be resolved.

Gramsci had brought out the important role played by culture in social change and social integration, arguing for its relative autonomy from the economic and political structures of modern society. What is striking in Gramsci's analysis is the stress placed on the normative elements of culture, the ways in which cultural practices work to socialise individuals, not as passive dupes of a dominant social system but as active agents who, having internalised cultural values, concede legitimacy to the social order. Such a process is always critical: agents internalise values reflexively, possessing the capacity both to judge them critically and, through praxis, to generate possible alternatives. Thus Gramsci's Marxism differs quite sharply from that of the

Frankfurt School. Culture industry stands above society, working downwards, as ideology dominating the consciousness of the broad mass: there is no sense of culture exercising a normative role or of agents actively interpreting and reflexively acting to shape the social world. Hence Adorno's problems, noted above, of theorising context in relation to both collective and individual agents.

In contrast to Gramsci, orthodox Marxist cultural theory (Lukács, Antal and Hauser) identified cultural production directly with class interests, with cultural forms conceived as expressions of the 'mentality' or the ideology of specific social groups or classes. A Marxist theory of culture became tied to a reductive notion of culture as a reflex of economic and ideological interests, with a false division established between the spheres of material production and those of the superstructure. A major problem lay in establishing the nature of links between these two spheres, the mechanisms whereby the material elements became transposed into ideal, cultural forms; and conversely, in demonstrating the passage of the 'ideal' to the 'real'. Orthodox Marxism solved this dualism by its assumption that the process was one of direct transmission (the standpoint of 'correspondences' and reflection), which effectively denied a Marxist theory of a materialist category of culture. For if cultural forms are mere reflections of other more fundamental forces then they can exercise little if any material existence of their own. As epiphenomena they lack all autonomy and materiality. Thus if culture is defined as embodying universal truth and alternative and oppositional values, as Adorno suggests, then its empirical and material reality becomes vague and insubstantial. Raymond Williams's theory of cultural materialism begins explicitly from this argument, that far from enjoying an excess of materialism Marxist cultural theory suffers from a 'deficit'.

The theory of cultural materialism is a theory of contextualisation. It seeks to establish a bridge between the immanent critique of critical theory (mediation through the social whole) and the more objective, historically grounded analysis of Gramsci (culture as the field of social struggles). Williams argues that the most characteristic features of cultural theory and analysis lie in 'the exploration and specification of distinguishable cultural formations', with the task of cultural materialism defined as the 'analysis of the specific relationships through which works are made and move' (Williams, 1989, pp. 173–4). In setting out to clarify the basic principles of Marxist cultural theory

Williams focusses on the category of specificity, to ask what is it which distinguishes one cultural form from non-cultural forms. As for the links between the cultural and the social, they require grasping as modes of practice in that both economic and cultural production involve complex forms of action. Williams follows Gramsci in identifying culture as practices which unite base and superstructure: culture is not a mirror of production but a mode of productive practice itself.

Culture as Ordinary: The Problem of a Common Culture

Raymond Williams's work on cultural theory spans the period from the 1940s to the 1980s, when he first developed the theory of cultural materialism. His early writings, notably *Culture and Society* (1955) and *The Long Revolution* (1961), had explored the concept of culture largely from within the discourses of English literary theory, media studies (especially film and television) and English fiction. Williams defined culture in terms of a broad and democratic tradition rooted in the particularity of English society. His aim, as he put it, was to wrest the concept of culture from the narrow and ultimately impoverished elitist usages it had assumed in English literary and cultural studies. An elitist notion of culture was especially marked in the work of the literary critic F.R. Leavis and the poet, dramatist and critic T.S. Eliot.

In England the debate on the meaning of culture had largely turned on the distinction established by nineteenth-century writers such as Matthew Arnold and John Ruskin, between culture as a realm of ideal values (nobility of purpose, beauty of forms) and the non-culture of an industrial society increasingly defined as mechanical and dehumanised. Modern industrialism was seen as promoting a mass, semi-literate public whose cultural aspirations were satisfied in the 'cheap thrills and sensations' of popular fiction and newspapers. What Arnold called 'people with a low standard of life' would inevitably come to dominate modern culture, instigating an inexorable lowering of standards.

In a work such as *Mass Civilisation and Minority Culture* (1930) Leavis followed this narrow concept of culture, although in his later studies of the English novel and poetry the analysis is broadened to encompass the place of culture within the social and historical framework of industrial society. While Leavis's work has largely been dismissed as subjective and elitist (based on his assumption of a canon of great writers and novels building to a 'great tradition' appreciated only by a small, educated reading public with critical sensitivities), it sought to contextualise culture (and literature) within a distinctive socio-historical structure. Culture was defined in terms of popular traditions, a sense of community and place, with the lives of ordinary people identified as the bedrock of authentic values standing opposed to the prevailing values of an urban, mass-industrial society. Writers who belonged to 'the great tradition' were those whose work resonated the popular culture of pre- and early industrial society: the novels of George Eliot and D.H. Lawrence, for example, furnished material on the existence of a viable national and common culture, providing meaning and purpose to human relationships increasingly threatened by the forces of modern industrialism. Culture linked different individuals into an 'organic community', into a national culture built around tradition and historical continuity. But in modern mass society this notion of culture as a whole way of life is threatened as mass-produced film, radio and popular fiction erode the links between an active common culture and literary creation.

As with the Frankfurt School, Leavis's work suggests that modern mass culture cannot play an active normative role. A fragmented and atomistic culture must inevitably lead to the decline of a genuine 'living tradition' in literature and the collapse of a coherent, educated and influential reading public. With the extension of the division of labour, work becomes increasingly specialised and isolating; the modern mass media function to undermine what remains of the organic link between everyday life and common cultural values. T.S. Eliot (in his *The Idea of a Christian Society*, 1939, and *Notes Towards a Definition of Culture*, 1948) linked culture with continuity and tradition, defining it as 'a way of feeling and acting' which characterises different social groups and generations; and while many of its elements remain unconscious, culture effectively defines the ways in which individuals act and grasp the social world: culture includes the whole range of a community's practices, a structure corresponding with the broader forces and patterns of 'society as a whole'. Like Leavis and Adorno, Eliot saw in the development of a bureaucratic and uniform mass society a powerful threat to creative cultural values (Shusterman, 1993).

Although the Leavis–Eliot paradigm theorised culture as 'experience' of the everyday world, grounding it in the historical–social context (in effect, a social definition of culture was advanced), Williams argued that both Leavis and Eliot exemplified an idealistic and highly selective tradition of cultural criticism, which failed to go beyond 'received' traditions of individual human beings as 'masses'. In both *Culture and Society* and *The Long Revolution* he sought to refute the theory that culture necessarily opposed the historical development of modern mass democracy, socialism and the working-class movement by proposing its basis in industrialism and popular democracy. Williams locates the origins of the modern usage of the term culture at the end of the eighteenth century, arguing that its emergence was not merely a response to the onset of industrial capitalism but closely linked with newly emerging social relationships and political institutions based around political democracy and the problems of social class. The difficulty with Eliot's 'selective' notion of culture was that it effectively separated culture from the broader structural developments of modern society, producing a false antinomy between cultural values and those of everyday life. In contrast, Williams suggested that culture was always 'ordinary', a form of 'lived experience', 'a whole way of life' and that the study of culture never implied a concept of a closed tradition but rather the possibilities of openness and democracy. He sharpened the Leavis–Eliot paradigm by analysing culture as the means whereby individuals communicated freely with each other. Culture was, therefore, not a thing in itself, an 'autonomous realm' existing outside other 'spheres' such as economics and politics, but bound up with the ordinary everyday world. Williams noted the largely negative connotations of the terms as applied to mass education and mass democracy, its pejorative usage reinforcing the division between a minority and a mass popular culture. On the contrary, he declared:

> There are, in fact, no masses; there are only ways of seeing people as masses. In an urban industrial society there are many opportunities for such ways of seeing. The point is not to reiterate the objective conditions but to consider, personally and collectively what these have done to our thinking...a way of seeing other people...characteristic of our kind of society, has been capitalised for the purpose of political or cultural exploitation. (Williams, 1961, p. 289)

As there are no empirically existing masses, so culture, as a way of life, was not reducible to such terms as 'intellectual growth' or 'states of mind'.

In *The Long Revolution* Williams sketched out a linear theory of social development in which both the industrial and democratic revolutions of the nineteenth century were closely bound up with a third, cultural revolution. Distinct from the economic and political revolutions, the cultural embraced the immense potential for new modes of communication, mass literacy, the growth of public education and the democratising of the mass media. Williams depicts an almost automatic process of democratic expansion involving education, communication and community in which the struggle for a common culture constitutes a powerful presence. By the long revolution he meant the aspirations to extend the 'active process' of learning to all social groups as well as seeking a more participatory democracy (Williams, 1965, p. 118). 'We need a common culture', he wrote, 'not for the sake of an abstraction, but because we shall not survive without it.' For industrial capitalism is built on the basis of social inequality, class conflict and social crisis. A common culture provides equal access to the varied and rich potential of human society. There can never be an absolute contrast, then, between the idea of minority culture and a broad humanist and democratic culture.

Writing in the 1950s, Williams was equally critical of Marxist attempts to define and theorise culture, dismissing them as simply 'confused'. The chapter on 'Marxism and Culture' in *Culture and Society* explicitly rejected the mechanistic base – superstructure model characteristic of contemporary Marxism (a model which compared badly with the autonomy given to culture in the Leavis–Eliot paradigm) in which culture becomes an effect of economic production and class ideologies. Yet, while critiquing and rejecting Marxism for its reductionism and failure to contextualise adequately, Williams advanced a reductionism of his own, assimilating the concept of culture to the institutions and practices of communication. Rather like Habermas (see Chapter 4), Williams suggests that culture stands behind the backs of those participating in relations of communication. Moreover, this concept of culture is sundered both from social struggles and power relations, so that 'who' questions are effectively ignored. Which specific groups and class are involved in the production and reproduction of culture; and which interests are at stake? Williams is not theorising culture sociologically but working within a literary theoretical framework close to Leavis. While recognising the importance of 'patterns, correspondences and discontinuities' in the relations between the various elements that comprise 'a whole way of life', Williams's concept of culture is uniform and cohesive, marginalising struggles over cultural resources, institutions and forms.

The Structure of Feelings: Problems of Contextualisation

Williams theorises culture non-teleologically (there is no 'dying culture'), defines it institutionally (especially its relation with education) and societally (through participation in a common culture). A culture by its nature assumes common, shared meanings in a state of development. In opposition to the mass culture thesis he rejects the conformism model of a uniform and passive mass wholly incorporated into modern capitalism.

Although emphasising the materiality of culture and its embodiment in collectivist institutions such as trade unions, Williams offers few analytical concepts for linking class, ideology, cultural production and reproduction empirically with the socio-historical context, defining culture in vague, ahistorical categories and abstractions such as solidarity, common needs and communication. Culture comes to constitute not only a body of 'intellectual and imaginative work' but also 'a whole way of life'. Such holistic, anthropological notions have the effect of assimilating culture to social practices and blur the distinction between culture and non-culture, culture and society. A major weakness in Williams's approach lies in establishing the principle of autonomy.

As we have seen, the Leavis–Eliot paradigm emphasised the principle of autonomy by linking culture with the creative, living values of popular community and tradition, defining it as ideal and critical. But in materialising his categories does Williams succeed in establishing a viable sociological concept of autonomy? For Williams, autonomy does not arise out of social institutions and social structure, rather it develops 'ideally', with its basis firmly rooted in the ideas of a particular historical period. The key element in this analysis is the structure of feelings, a concept common to Williams's early and later Marxist work. In *Marxism and Literature* (1977) and *Problems in Materialism and Culture* (1980) he stressed the importance of reconceptualising Marxist analysis by locating culture at the level of the material social process and by rethinking Marxist categories such as hegemony, mode of production, totality and mediation.

The structure of feeling, however, links the social notion of culture as communication and practices, with culture as imaginative art and literature. Williams defines it as the culture of a particular period, 'the particular living result of all the elements in the general organisation'. Every historical period is characterised by patterns of impulses, restraints and tones with relationships formed between them. From such elements 'useful cultural analysis' begins, sometimes yielding up 'unexpected identities and correspondences'. Thus, discussing the industrial novels published in England during the turbulent 1840s, Williams identifies a largely middle-class structure of feeling in which class values dominate. On the one hand, writers such as Mrs Gaskell and Charles Kingsley were critical of the deleterious social effects of industrialism, expressing deep sympathy with the working class, but on the other they remained apart, distancing themselves from any social and political involvement. At the same time, this structure of feeling was shared by other contemporary working-class writers and in this way important links were forged between different groups and similar literary forms (Williams, 1965, pp. 63–88).

Williams defines the structure of feelings as 'a very deep and wide possession, in all actual communities . . . One generation may train its successors . . . in the social character of the general cultural pattern, but the next generation will have its own structure of feeling'. The concept is specifically aimed at generations and he cites the example of the 1930s writers (Auden, Isherwood, Spender and MacNeice) as a distinctive generation producing new cultural work, a group with a median age of around thirty years 'when it is beginning to articulate its structure of feeling'. Although a structure of feeling is realised only through 'the experiences of the work of art itself', the concept focusses on the ways in which social and historical relations express themselves through language and form within the texts. However, to situate a text in its context never 'exhausts' its range of meanings and values, because there is always some element 'for which there is no external counterpart' (Williams, 1979, pp. 157–68).

As an explanation for autonomy this is vague and slippery. For although the structure of feeling is defined as historically specific, at times it approaches epochal analysis, floating free of material forces, especially social structure and institutions. In particular, the structure of feelings tends to flatten out the social space in which different social groups of writers and artists move. Culture does not automatically translate itself into art and literature, conventions and forms. If a similar structure of feelings informs the work of both middle and working-class writers then it is essential to analyse the precise ways and mechanisms through which this process occurs. The structure of feelings cannot translate itself into a sociological concept unless it is firmly anchored in some notion of social structure. If it is to function as a sociological category then it must uncover the links between disparate structures, values and feelings, and social groups, language and social structure, the sources of potential conflict and competition between different groups, and examine the ways social groups may appropriate culture as forms of domination.

Williams's claim that as an integral part of his theory of cultural materialism the concept forms the basis for a theory of autonomy is clearly untenable; the structure of feelings is inadequately contextualised, approximating to a correspondence theory in which all the complex structures are simplified and flattened out. The basic problem lies in Williams's general model of culture as a process dominated by depersonalised rather than living, historical forces. There is no sense of culture and cultural change bound up with social struggles and issues of power. Rather, Williams presents a sense of the past evolving unproblematically into the present, emptied of the very real conflicts within the culture of the past, which continue to live in, and shape, the present, 'the present as history'. Williams's concept of culture and mode of analysis are inadequate to deal with culture's living historical forms. Perhaps the real problem lies in theorising culture as 'a way of life', which suggests both its passive nature and lack of autonomy.

To resolve these problems, Williams introduces the concepts of hegemony and the social formation as a structure of distinct levels. In *The Long Revolution* and *Culture and Society* there was no attempt to define society or social structure in anything other than abstractly historical terms. But in his later work, Williams assimilates a structuralist Marxist concept of society as a social formation into his cultural model in ways consistent with the principle of autonomy. Rejecting the concept of a linear process in cultural change, he argues that no mode of production, social order and culture can ever exhaust 'all human practice, human energy and human intention'. There is no total incorporation (Williams, 1977, p. 125).

The theory of cultural materialism breaks from the 'empiricist' approach of Williams's early work with its basis in experience

(Leavis's 'lived experience' as the touchstone of authenticity) to analyse culture as a process of material production, 'a signifying system'
through which the social order is 'communicated, reproduced, experienced and explored' (Williams, 1981, pp. 12–13). Cultural materialism
is defined as

> a theory of culture, as a [social and material] productive process and of
> specific practices, of 'arts', as social uses of material means of production
> [from language as material] 'practical consciousness' to the specific tech-
> nologies of writing and forms of writing, through to mechanical and
> electronic communication systems. (Williams, 1989, p. 243).

The introduction of the term 'practice' into Williams's vocabulary
suggests a more active concept of culture. He argues that cultural
materialism demands a notion of mediation, one which goes beyond
the passivity implicit in all reflectionist models to focus on the making
of meanings and values within specific historical contexts. As a theory
of the specifics of material and cultural production, cultural materialism moves beyond the downwards conflation of orthodox Marxism
by developing the concepts of hegemony and structural levels.

For Williams, hegemony constitutes a major turning point in Marxist cultural theory, in that it challenges many of the dominant theoretical assumptions of orthodox Marxism such as homology and
correspondence, with their basis in reflectionism and economic determinism. Although, as I have suggested above, Williams had implicitly
used these terms in his previous work, he argues that the concept of
hegemony goes beyond a narrow definition of culture to an emphasis
on the whole social process by introducing crucial issues of social
struggles and power. Moreover, it goes beyond ideology in that hegemony is never merely a question of class outlook, or the world-view of
a particular class, but rather a structure which embraces a whole body
of practices and expectations, energy, perceptions and a lived system
of values and meanings. Nor is hegemony mere superstructure: it
constitutes a lived process, a rich, deep, thorough, realised complex
of experiences, relations and action, a process in which needs are
continually renewed, recreated, defended and modified.

It will be evident that Williams has defined hegemony in culturalist
terms as a lived process built around practices, values and needs. As I
argued in Chapter 2, Gramsci's concept of hegemony focused on the
specific structural basis of culture, on the complex balance of forces

within specific social contexts and the struggles arising out of the relations between social groups and classes. Analytically, hegemony enables the researcher to grasp the links between institutions, ideologies and collective agents, to theorise culture as a mobile field of forces rooted in specific relations of production. Hegemony is thus a particular mode of theorising contexts: but in his analysis of socio-cultural contexts, Williams employs the structuralist notion of levels, identifying three distinct levels of cultural production: the residual (largely consisting of the culture of the past which continues to lead an active life in the present and is, therefore, not necessarily archaic), the emergent (newly developing practices, meanings and values which can be oppositional or provide alternatives to the dominant culture) and, finally, the dominant (which reaches widely into many practices and experiences, seeking to incorporate alternative and oppositional values).

In these formulations Williams is striving to move away from epochal analysis, the assumption of a single, overarching cultural pattern to a particular social formation (i.e. the idea that bourgeois culture necessarily corresponds to bourgeois capitalism). In short, that cultural analysis must recognise the significance of internal differentiation and complexity. He makes the point, for example, that no dominant culture can successfully eliminate other practices, but equally the dominant culture of modern capitalism has penetrated more significantly 'into the whole social and cultural process', creating problems for emergent and oppositional values (Williams, 1977, pp. 125–6).

Is this a reversal to a dominant ideology thesis, a modified version of culture industry? In what ways and by what mechanisms do the different levels Williams has identifies exert any autonomy? The problem with cultural materialism is that it offers no systematic means of grounding its concepts contextually: hegemony seems to hover enigmatically over the whole culture with vague appeals to practices, lived experience and struggle. Structural levels are similarly analysed in vague, abstract terms. Williams's mode of theorising, originating from literary studies, hardly changes from *Culture and Society* to *Marxism and Literature*. The problems of contextualisation are inadequately raised. There is no attempt to analyse the links between the different levels of a cultural formation and its varied practices; the question of micro and macro analysis is subordinated to general concepts as 'lived experiences' and 'a whole social process'.

Williams fails to address the fundamental problem of social struggles between different social classes, fractions of classes and groups, and the role these play in the creation of culture and cultural forms. The concepts of cultural materialism are so many abstractions, emptied of historical flesh and blood and disengaged from historical and socio-logical contextualisation.

Chapter 6

The Theory of Cultural Fields

One of the fundamental theoretical problems of Marxist theories of culture lay in their failure to grasp the specifics of cultural production – the principle of autonomy and the dependent relations with other elements of the social context. Williams's cultural materialism, while addressing these issues, fails to elucidate those specific components which distinguish culture from other elements of the social formation. The principle of the autonomy of culture is made problematic through collapsing culture into the social, 'a way of life'. There is, too, the tendency to reduce texts either to an abstractly rendered notion of social context (and the assumption that social background translates itself unproblematically into the foreground) or to the expression of particular cultural groups. And while acknowledging that struggle and conflict play a role in the formation of culture, Williams fails to specify precisely the nature of such forces. Thus, while claiming its basis in humanism, cultural materialism significantly raises no question of the making of culture, of who, how and why. The historical or genetic is subsumed under terms such as communication, while hegemony is drained of all living historical forces.

Structuralism and the Concept of System

In developing his theory of cultural materialism, Williams identified the influence of Gramsci but equally that of structuralism and Russian formalism (especially the literary theorists Tynyanov and Bakhtin). Both formalism and structuralism raised the problem of autonomy and contextualisation. Formalism, with its focus on literature and 'literariness' as its defining property, emphasised the internal specifics of literary forms, especially the use of poetic language and specific devices of plot and story (components of form) to the exclusion of extraliterary factors; and structuralism grounded the notion of form through a concept of a dynamically integrated whole in which the different elements interact with each other. It was Tynyanov who theorised the concept of literary system as a structural process, a complex whole in which the different elements are dynamically inter-related and play constructive functions. In his article 'Literary Evolution' (1927) Tynyanov conceived system in both synchronic and diachronic modes:

> The very concept of a continuously evolving synchronic system is contra-dictory. A literary system is first of all a system of the functions of the literary order which are in continual interrelationship with other orders. Systems change in their composition but ... the evolution of literature, as of other cultural systems, does not coincide either in tempo or in character with the systems with which it is interrelated. This is owing to the specificity of the material with which it is concerned. (Tynyanov, 1978, p. 72)

It is this concept of 'specificity' which echoes Weber's principle of autonomy. But Tynyanov goes beyond Weber by theorising the rela-tions between one system (Weber's spheres) and other, 'neighbouring' systems. Moreover, he demonstrates the autonomy of systems in terms of history – the evolution of literature, a complex process involving the immanent formal elements of literary forms as they develop unevenly in relation to other systems. Tynyanov further argues that literary evolution is non-linear, characterised by 'struggle and succession' as one literary form, or genre, succeeds another, transforming the existing hierarchy and canons (the order and author-ity of different literary genres and texts).

One of the problems with Tynyanov's formulations is the nature of the extraliterary systems and their relations with the literary system itself. Tynyanov seems to define neighbouring systems not as objective cultural wholes but rather as 'texts' (for example, the widespread social convention of letter writing, which over time became an ele-ment of the literary system introduced through the epistolary novel) and the whole system as 'intertextual' – that is, one made up of different forms of writing (fictional and non-fictional) and the codes or discourses which circulate at specific periods. In the theorising of the literary system as 'inter-textual' (Tynyanov does not use this term, Julia Kristeva introduced it in the 1960s), the influence of social forces on the genesis and structure of the literary system is unclear: the concept of struggle, for example, is described as immanent to the system with no extra-system reference. If changes occur they do so internally, through a process of modification and adjustment to extra-literary material. As an example, Tynyanov frequently cited the influence of so-called 'hybrid' genres, – memoirs and reportage, for example – on literary evolution but without specifying the exact mechanisms which facilitate the transition from extraliterary to literary. System, for Tynyanov, develops and functions without choices, values and motivation. Who makes choices, why and how are they realised? The diachronic element is system-induced. In contrast, Gramsci's theory of hegemony, which shares some of the features of Tynyanov's concept of system, does not reduce culture to 'texts', and conceives its transformation in terms of collective agents and the relations between distinct classes and social groups.

In the development of structuralism, however, Tynyanov's diachronic approach became subordinated to an increasing concentration on an anti-genetic and anti-historical concept of structure. More problematically, the whole question of contexualisation was reduced to highly abstract and formalist analyses of patterns, sequences and differences within culture. Bourdieu's theory of fields represents the most serious attempt to recover the principles of specificity, autonomy and contextualism implicit in Tynyanov's model (similar to the 'internal logic' of Weber's spheres) by integrating them within an historical–sociological theory of culture.

Cultural Theory and the Short Circuit Effect

The basic problem inherent in structuralism lay in its attack on the idea of a constituting socio-cultural context (as a form of reductionism) and the elimination of the active role of agent (as a form of subjectivism). For Bourdieu, the strength of structuralism lay in its 'objectivism', with its weaknesses in a failure to deal with crucial issues of consciousness, practice and agency. Sartre's existentialism, with its focus on the consciousness of agents and criticism of mechanistic Marxism, constituted the other intellectual tradition influencing

Bourdieu's cultural sociology. Bourdieu was quite adamant that it was not a question of making a choice between objectivism and subjectivism but rather one of preserving the gains of both structuralism and existentialism. His task was to unify the subjective and objective in sociological analysis (Bourdieu and Wacquant, 1992, p. 135). Between the objective and the subjective lies a complex structure of forces which become ignored, or have their role minimised, if direct and immediate links are established between cultural artefacts and specific features of the social context (the cultural producers, social groups and social location). Bourdieu calls this the 'short circuit effect' and includes as examples the Marxist studies of Antal, Hauser and Lucien Goldmann together with the Frankfurt School, all of whom exemplify an 'external' mode of analysis, attributing the genesis of cultural forms to the world view, ideology or patronage of specific groups or classes.

For Bourdieu it was not a question of isolating a social group and linking it directly with cultural production, but rather one of analysing the complex set of relations existing between social groups, artists and society. Artistic production does not take place in isolation from other forms of cultural activity, but is imbricated in a whole network and field of artistic production as a whole.

Antal's study of Florentine Rennaisance painting represents an exemplary work which links cultural forms directly with patronage of the nascent commercial bourgeoisie. But by focusing on the social group as the source of creative activity, Antal assumes a direct transposition of this group's ideology into artistic work. Thus culture and art are theorised as expressions of outside forces. Similarly, Goldmann's study of Racine and Pascal, *The Hidden God*, is criticised by Bourdieu for identifying and linking a specific world view, the 'tragic vision', with the economic and political fate of a specific social class, the *noblesse de robe* an emerging but marginal bourgeois formation. Both Goldmann and Antal fail to specify the complex play of forces at work within 'the universe of artistic production', with its particular traditions and the laws which regulate its workings, recruitment and history. The autonomy of art is no more than the relative autonomy of this structure, or field, and the sociology of culture must, therefore,

take as its object the whole set of relationships (objective ones and also those effected in the form of interactions) *between the artist and other*

artists, and beyond them, the whole set of agents engaged in the production
of work or, at least, of the *social value* of the work (critics, gallery directors,
patrons, etc.). (Bourdieu, 1993a, p. 140; Bourdieu's emphasis)

Cultural sociology must, therefore, move beyond defining social
context in terms of background, or milieu, and linking cultural production to the socialisation and education of artists and writers, their
social origins or the ideology of their patrons. It is especially false to
identify cultural production with the structure and values of particular
social groups, because such relations offer no more than 'accidental'
or 'additional' information:

> It is the field of artistic production as a whole (which stands in a relation of
> relative autonomy greater or lesser depending on the period and the
> society, with respect to the groups from which the consumers of its pro-
> ducts are recruited i.e. the various fractions of the ruling class). (ibid.,
> p. 142)

For Bourdieu, there is no final or efficient cause which determines the
content and form of art.

It may seem paradoxical that Bourdieu lumps together in one
category such diverse Marxist cultural theorists as Antal, Goldmann
and Adorno, for ostensibly their work is rigorously opposed to the
mechanistic formulations associated with the short circuit effect. The
case of Adorno seems particularly problematic. As we have seen, his
work is grounded in an analysis of culture informed by Marx's materialism and Weber's thesis of the differentiation of spheres. Adorno was
especially critical, for example, of the short circuit effect implicit in
Walter Benjamin's study of Baudelaire and nineteenth-century Paris,
the 'Arcades Project', in which relations of correspondence were
advanced between changes occurring in capitalist economic forms in
the late nineteenth century (towards the total dominance in economic
life of the commodity form) and those within culture and consciousness. In his analysis of Baudelaire's poetry, for example, Benjamin
advocated a homologous relation between the specificity of the poetic
image and the structure of capitalist commodity production, the commodity form becoming directly transmuted into what he called 'dialectical images', so that the figures who populate the poetry, the
flaneur, the stroller and the idler of the Parisian streets, correspond
directly with the new forms of architecture, notably the shopping

arcades. In short, the social context is inscribed within literary and cultural forms as 'fragments', as fleeting experiences in a new, urban environment.

This obvious short circuit effect – art as the expression of the primacy of technology and developments in artificial building material – drew from Adorno the comment that Benjamin's method lacked genuine dialectics: 'Throughout your text there is a tendency to relate the pragmatic contents of Baudelaire's work immediately to adjacent features in the social history of his time, preferably economic features.' Benjamin failed to analyse 'the mediation through the total social process', proposing rather a strict and thus narrowly conceived correlation between artistic images and economic production (Adorno, 1973).

However, Adorno's recourse to the category of mediation, while avoiding the reductionism of mechanistic Marxism and the problem of the short circuit effect, fails to resolve the critical issue of sociological contextualisation: to advocate analysis based on the concept of a universal mediation through the category of totality and the ways artistic forms present images of an 'antagonistic society' is to commit the error of cutting off the complex play of forces at work within the processes of cultural production. What is missing in Adorno's formulation is a sociological category of mediation, one which deals with the specific, relatively autonomous 'spaces' within cultural production involving institutions, agents and practices. For Bourdieu, the solution to the 'short circuit effect' lies in developing a more complex, because historically specific, notion of sociocultural context, one which takes account of diversity and difference, hierarchical structures within production and consumption, conflict and struggles over cultural resources and status. To produce culture implies a whole network of relations which function at different levels (between different producers and consumers), involving differences of power and status, generations and new conceptions of artistic form.

Context is historical and specific: Tynyanov's literary system, for example, fails to deal with the social and historical basis of art forms or the historical dynamic underpinning the genesis and transformations of the system itself and its artefacts. It is precisely against the internalist and externalist reductionisms that Bourdieu develops this theory of fields.

Cultural Sociology and the Concept of Field

Bourdieu defines social context as multidimensional space differentiated into distinct fields, networks of objective positions occupied by agents through their possession of different forms of capital—economic (material skills, wealth), cultural (knowledge, intellectual skills) and symbolic (accumulated prestige and sense of honour). A field is thus

> a configuration, of objective relations between positions...objectively defined, in their existence and in the determinations they impose upon their occupants, agents or institutions, by their present and potential situation in the structure of the distribution of species of power (or capital) whose possession commands access to the specific profits that are at stake in the field, as well as their objective relation to other positions (domination, subordination, homology, etc.). (Bourdieu and Wacquant, 1992, p. 97)

The concept of field constitutes the 'true object of social science', a structured 'space of positions' and not a nominalist unity of isolated individuals, a system of power lines, a 'magnetic' field, to be analysed both genetically (historically) and synchronically (its internal structure). Education, the state, church, political parties and the arts are thus fields in Bourdieu's terms (and not ideological apparatuses standing above and dominating society), partly autonomous 'spheres' (close to Weber's differentiation thesis) characterised by an internal specific logic which belongs to the field itself. Thus the literary field is dynamically structured through differences which form a system 'of distinctive and antagonistic properties which do not develop out of their own internal motion...but via conflicts internal to the field of production'. To contextualise the study of literature, therefore, is to situate it within 'relations of force' and 'struggles' which aim to transform both the relations between different agents and positions and the literary field as a whole (ibid., p. 104).

All fields have their own specific internal logic of laws, but they share a general law: those occupying dominant positions will necessarily adopt defensive and conservative 'conservation strategies' in order to preserve their status. And, in contrast, newcomers will develop 'subversion strategies' seeking to overthrow the rules governing the field while, at the same time, accepting its legitimacy. This is effectively the precondition for entry to any field, a recognition of 'values at stake' (the 'spirit of the game') and thus the limits to criticism. Hence all internal struggles within fields eventuate in 'partial' and not total revolutions, in action which destroys an existing hierarchy 'but not the game itself'. A revolution in the artistic field, for example, will challenge established definitions and practices in the name of a purer art, film or literature, 'shaking up' the structure of the field while leaving its legitimacy intact (Bourdieu, 1993a, p. 134).

As I have noted, Bourdieu's field concept is broadly similar to Weber's theory of differentiated spheres – relatively autonomous social microcosms characteristic of modern complex societies. The relative autonomy of fields is a slow and piecemeal process built up over many years as they establish their own specific institutions, rules and practices. Unlike Weber, Bourdieu theorises fields dynamically in terms of their transformative properties, the strategies employed by the different agents in the struggles for legitimacy. Through the volume and distribution of the different forms of capital, agents are endowed and provided with the capacities to participate in such struggles: '*A capital does not exist and function except in relation to a field.*' It confers a power over the field, over the materialised or embodied instruments of production or reproduction whose distribution constitutes the very structure of the field...' (ibid., p. 101, Bourdieu's emphasis).

Bourdieu's theory of fields is further indebted to the relational thinking of structuralism, in that fields are defined as 'systems of relations that are independent of the populations which these relations define', objective relations existing independently of human consciousness. The 'structuralist revolution', he argued, 'identifies the real not with substances but with relations', not with realist notions such as 'groups' or 'classes', with fixed characteristics and definable properties, but with objective relations existing between groups and classes. It is not a question of the interactions between elements, because these 'conceal the structures that are realised in them'. And as fields are never static and finished but are always in a process of 'making', the products of action, relational analysis alone explains how agents act through their relations with others. Relations, like fields, are always in a state of change, unfinalised and striving to transform both the agent and the situation. In this sense, the 'stuff of the social is made of relations', not of individuals or substances (ibid., pp. 106, 179, 197; Bourdieu, 1990, p. 127). However, the weakness of this form of structuralist objectivism is its tendency to reify the concept of structure. Relational theorising must incorporate a subjectivist dimension, one which includes a concept of the agent as active, creative and imaginative.

For Bourdieu, structuralism lacks an adequate theory of practice; the agent is dominated by the structure existing as a support or function of the hidden rules of discourse. In this sense, structuralist concepts of system tend to be a closed rather than open form and there is little, if any, dialogical communication occurring between the various levels or positions. Structuralism fails to account for 'culturally mediated action', which lies at the heart of Bourdieu's cultural sociology. Equally, structuralism ignores the historical nature of action, that fields and agents are the products of history. To adopt a structuralist model of field is to situate the agent and his or her actions as the passive products of determinate objective relations, but not to examine the precise ways and the elements involved in action itself. Relational thinking must be enriched by theorising the distinctive properties which motivate different courses of action within specific fields. This is Bourdieu's methodological jumping-off point from the structuralist revolution: an analysis of the subjective sources of action through the concept of habitus.

Habitus, Practices and the Cultural Fields

A field consists of a space of possibilities, a balance of forces subsisting between different agents engaged in struggles and competition. It is not intersubjective ties between agents which structure a field, but objectively defined relations between different positions.

What, then, is the role allocated to agents in the construction of fields? How successful is Bourdieu in combining the objectivist concept of field with a subjectivist notion of action? In what ways are agents the producers of fields? And in emphasising relationism over interactionism, how does Bourdieu explain both the genesis and the transformation of the structure and the agent?

Bourdieu argues that it is the internal structure of a field which enables agents to act and transform relations. Unlike an apparatus (an extreme, pathological form of a field), fields develop through the practices of active, not passive, agents. Bourdieu makes the point that agents are socialised into distinctive fields, not through norms but cognitively through internalising the social structure of the field itself. In short, the agent transposes the objective structure of a field (the hierarchy of positions, traditions, institutions, history) into 'mental structures', or frameworks, which then work to condition the ways the field is perceived, grasped and understood, and the possibilities for action inherent within it.

To act, however, requires more than these cognitive frameworks. Agents make choices over this or that course of action, over whether to engage in practices which may transform both the field and themselves. Bourdieu employs the notion of habitus, 'socialised subjectivity', meaning not a habit but a system of 'durable dispositions' or properties, which allow agents to understand, interpret and act in the social world. Habitus both organises practices and allows for the perception of practices.

The concept of habitus derived originally from Panofsky's study of Gothic art and his theory of a homologous relationship between Gothic architecture and certain basic principles of the medieval common culture. Based on the thirteenth-and fourteenth-century scholastic philosophy taught at the major educational institutions, these principles effectively became the internalised 'master patterns' underpinning the mental habits that governed the aesthetics of Gothic architecture. Such patterns constitute a structural homology between different forms of intellectual activity, architecture, the Gothic cathedrals and philosophy (Bourdieu, 1971, pp. 82–5).

Noting that both Durkheim and Mauss developed a broadly similar approach to linking mental structures with social structures, Bourdieu defines habitus as the acquired, autonomous and permanent set of dispositions which, durably incorporated in the body, enable individuals to adapt and adjust to widely differing contexts. Neither coordinated nor governed by specific rules, habitus is inculcated in childhood and structured by the social context, becoming ingrained in the individual as both generative and transposable dispositions. Although the practices generated are unconscious (for example, the ways individuals walk, stand, eat and laugh) habitus is not automatic, mechanical or repetitive, but the

> capacity for generating practices or utterances or works... in no way innate and is historically constituted... not completely reducible to its conditions of productions not least because it functions in a *systematic* way... The

habitus is a principle of invention produced by history but relatively
detached from history... (Bourdieu, 1993a, p. 87)

Habitus assumes a reflexive agent whose orientation to the social
world is grounded in practical knowledge, and Bourdieu cites Marx
for the argument that between the 'conditions of existence' and the
variety of social practices the 'structuring activity' of human agents
intervenes. It is not a question of agents adapting passively to a social
world their actions have helped produce, but one of creative and
imaginative agents open to many possibilities, able to employ knowledge and skills in maintaining and advancing their social position
within fields. Moreover, agents act through 'practical sense' in which
goals and ends are not determined solely through conscious, deliber-
ate and rational practice but flow from the socially constituted 'feel
for the game' (Bourdieu and Wacquant, 1992, p. 126).

Bourdieu's is not a finalising but an open-ended concept of practice, one in which a complex balance is maintained between a conscious strategy involving free choice, and non-conscious action based
on common identity and a shared culture of a common language
and sentiments. But choice is always circumscribed by the habitus
and the field: a reflexive agent is possible only under specific social
conditions:

> Social agents are the *product of history*, of the history of the whole social
> field and of the accumulated experience of a path within the specific sub-
> field... social agents will *actively* determine, on the basis of these socially
> and historically constituted categories of perception and appreciation, the
> situation that determines them. One can even say that social agents are
> determined only to the extent that they determine themselves. (Bourdieu,
> 1984, pp. 135–6)

The habitus is thus responsible for the ways in which individuals
classify and differentiate a whole range of cultural practices, from
painting and writing to sport and photography. On the latter, Bourdieu suggests that only approximately ten per cent of the population
have the necessary artistic and aesthetic dispositions to classify photography as an aesthetic rather than an everyday, utilitarian activity. The
principles which structure individual perceptions of photography are
bound up with class habitus, and practices imbricated in the structure
and relations of class society. Thus the working class use photography

in a strictly practical and functional mode to celebrate such rites of passage as marriage, birthdays and other significant cultural moments (Bourdieu, 1990b).

Similarly, in *Distinction* Bourdieu notes that working-class dispositions militate against radical and formalist experimentation in the arts in favour of mimetic and representational modes. Such practices are the products of the relation between habitus and field. Thus within the field of diplomacy the dispositions linked to an upper-class family background and a public school education enable individuals to integrate with confidence and style into a highly formalised social world dominated by pomp and official ceremony. So habitus, closely integrated with class and family, functions as a powerful conservative force binding individuals to the social order. Following Durkheim, Bourdieu argues that symbolic systems (such as distinctions relating to high and low culture, etc.) have the effect of reinforcing existing social distinctions by representing, in a 'misrecognised' form, the structure of class relations. Thus the ways in which different social classes classify cultural goods and practices as 'natural', and not socially constituted, are the product of habitus: the conclusion is profoundly conservative, namely that the working class accept their social position and status, with culture functioning to occlude perception and understanding of the social and historical roots of class domination (Bourdieu, 1984, pp. 249–50).

Thus habitus functions practically as 'structuring structures...as principles which generate and organise practices and representations'. Although they can be modified by later experiences, the system of dispositions become ingrained, internalised as 'second nature', a form of 'embodied history' which links the agents with their past. Habitus thus preserves a sense of continuity, working as non-conscious structuring principles which govern the ways the past plays an active role within the present. Each individual contains the individual of yesterday acquiring through past experiences the necessary capital that enables him or her to function within a specific field. The result is 'permanence in change', habitus as the active presence of the whole past, as well as the product itself of that past. Hence, Bourdieu's insistence that it is this sense of the past ('embodied history') the present as history and not the experience of immediacy (or the empirical everyday world) which constitutes the principle of autonomy of the habitus (Bourdieu, 1990a, pp. 52–6).

Bourdieu is thus advancing a radical, non-functionalist theory of habitus in which a subjectivist element is linked with cultural change and continuity. Although the logic of practice is common to a number of fields, it is through their accumulated capital that individuals can reduce competition and establish a monopoly over the field itself. By challenging the established order they seek to institute the 'new', but not as something which threatens the field's existence. For habitus generates a sense of continuity, so that the most radical groups accept the legitimacy of the field, its institutions and traditions and seek to avoid any rupture with its past. It is thus within the cultural field, in the subfields of music, literature and painting, that revolutions are always partial, interpreting the new art of the present in terms of both the structure of positions within a field (for the 'new' embodies the values of rising social groups, providing them with a distinctive cultural identity against those in established positions for whom art has been appropriated conservatively) and its dynamic relations with the past (the 'new' as a necessary development out of the past art in which continuity is strengthened by the specific appropriation and evaluations which are relevant to the present). Thus the most radical artistic tendencies – the Dadaist, Surrealist and Futurist movements, for example – rejected totally the legitimacy of the established artistic field (its concepts of art, aesthetic practices and cultural institutions), challenging it externally by developing its own artistic sphere. The history of such avant-garde movements suggests that these strategies are doomed to failure: to overthrow the dominant culture, the avant-garde must function within the existing artistic field and, far from producing a complete rupture from the past, establish an authoritative presence through a renewal of tradition. Similarly, contemporary minimalist music, with its insistence on the outmoded nature of classical forms and harmony, ostensibly synthesising the popular (the use of simple, commonplace units of two or three notes generating a repetitive and hypnotic effect similar to that of rock music) and the classical (using the genres of opera, symphony and concerto but challenging their intellectual structure) undermines the legitimacy of a musical field split into the serious and the popular: working through the major serious genres, minimalism seeks a renewal of the past by reinvigorating old forms with contemporary aesthetic relevance.

The cultural field, then, is structured in struggles over such issues as the status of a 'classic' and the dominant canons in theatrical and musical performance (for example, contemporary feminist critiques of art, which seek to establish a suppressed historical tradition of women writers, painters and composers). Bourdieu's model, while bringing together the subjectivist and objectivist bases of cultural production, runs the risk of overstating the role of social struggles in the genesis of new art forms. Cultural capital enables individuals to occupy specific positions within the cultural field, but struggle is not necessarily an integral part of the process of cultural creation. The concept of social struggles belongs more properly to the institutional infrastructure of a field (for example, publishing, performance, publicity, marketing, networks of economic, social and political alliances), with its basis in business and profit, within the organisation of art. And here there is likely to be a different habitus from that structuring the cultural producers, who are motivated by goals and practices linked to the specifics of art itself. Habitus, in short, may not be adequate to deal with the potential open nature of cultural practices, while the field concept is too rigid, enclosing the agents as it does within determining structures. Defining a field as a field of forces may represent an advance on mechanistic and reductionist notions of context, but the exact modes of struggle which provide its dynamic momentum must be clearly specified. There are likely to be different forms of struggle between different institutions over the production, promotion and reception of art, struggles between artists and those who seek to promote their work, struggle between artists working within the same movement: if the concept of force field, with its related notions of habitus and capital, is to have any analytical value for cultural sociology then these are the fundamental issues which require clarification.

The Concept of Force Field

In developing his theory of fields, Bourdieu acknowledged the influence of Michel Foucault, who 'rigorously formulated' the concept of 'discursive fields' in which the different discourses of punishment, medicine and sexuality defined themselves internally in relation to a system of differences and 'dispersions'. In Foucault's formulation, a field consists of partly autonomous discourses which refuse harmonious integration into a unified corpus of knowledge. Rejecting the 'global' analysis of Marxism and structuralism, with its concepts of totality and system, Foucault proposed the radical idea of discourses

developing unevenly lacking integrative links to the centre. Foucault's
field of differences is thus built around the principle of discontinuity,
plurality and decentred structure, focusing on micrological not macro-
logical forces. He rejected the externalist, reflectionist, reductionist
method of Marxism with its conflation of discourse, a micrological
form, with economic or class structure. By emphasising the internal
structure of discourse, Foucault was able to explain the coexistence of
different discourses existing independently of a dominant element.
Thus the field of discourse becomes a field of forces, different discourses with their distinctive identity and structure.

Bourdieu makes the point that Foucault's field of discourse is
broadly comparable with Tynyanov's literary system, a network of
relations between different texts, in which change occurs from within
and is not external to the field itself. Both Tynyanov and Foucault
separate discourse and its texts from the social conditions of production, so that change is located within the relation of texts to each other
(an example of the short circuit effect). For Bourdieu, fields are social
microcosms founded through both an internal logic and, simultaneously, the external logic of the socio-historical context.

Analytically, the field concept suggests a network of objective relations between different positions defined in terms of the distribution
of economic, cultural and symbolic capital. Fields are constructed
around issues of power, social struggles between classes, and fractions
of classes, each pursuing their own distinctive goals and strategies
which strive for cultural legitimacy. Fields are thus fields of struggle,
'force fields', which aim at transforming or maintaining the established balance of forces. In contrast, the concepts of system, apparatus
or culture industry, erode the dynamic principle of fields – struggle,
conflict, competititon, the active role of opposition and resistance –
for fields are never static, finished, frozen in time, but rather are
characterised by 'an open space of play' and fluid boundaries. While
fields are never wholly autonomous (the laws of the market exert
important external influences), the more they approach autonomy
the more completely they fulfil their internal potential. At the same
time, fields are historically specific, their internal differentiation and
rationality the products of particular historical developments,
grounded in time and space and not, as with some Marxist and
Parsonian systems theory, governed by transhistorical laws. The field
concept is thus linked with modernity, because less complex, undiffer-

entiated societies lack the 'uncoupling mechanisms' which enable fields to separate from centralised political, religious and ideological institutions (Calhoun, 1995, p. 177).

In analysing the complex ways fields work, Bourdieu emphasises that the sociological study of fields is both theoretical – critical and empirical – historical, since because fields are historically specific they must be reconstituted each time in research. Each field is unique. At the same time, Bourdieu is concerned with the general historical trend towards the autonomisation of fields and the mechanisms which result in change. In describing his standpoint as 'genetic structuralist', Bourdieu identifies the dynamic principle producing change as the relation of habitus to field, in which dispositions orientate agents to both past and present, as well as to specific reproductive strategies.

In his analysis of the French literary field in the second half of the nineteenth century, Bourdieu identifies a number of oppositions – art and money, aesthetically pure and commercial art, the dominant groups and the challengers – functioning within a field of struggle which seeks 'to preserve or transform the field of forces...' But how far does Bourdieu's model account for the active role of agent in this field of forces? In what ways do authors, for example, shape the structure of the field and transform specific genres through their own voluntaristic practice? Bourdieu's answer is that within a force field authors 'only exist and subsist under the structural constraints of the field', adopting specific aesthetic perspectives to distinguish their objective position from that of others. Agents exist only in terms of the position they occupy in a field, positions which may change as the field changes; over a span of time, agents may occupy different positions in relation to publishing houses, journal editing, membership of literary groups, etc. The agent (and his or her biography) has no autonomy outside the structure of positions and dispositions linked to them:

> It is within each state of the field, defined by a particular configuration of the structure of the possibles, that the dispositions linked to a certain social origin orient practice towards one or another of the 'possibles' offered as a function of the position which is occupied and of the more or less clearly avowed feeling of success or failure associated with it. (Bourdieu, 1993b, pp. 184–9; see also 1996, ch.1)

One of the basic problems with this model of force field and Bourdieu's concern with incorporating the actions of agents without slipping into various modes of determinism, is that it provides no adequate explanation for the specificity of cultural change. After all, why was it that Flaubert developed an entirely new kind of novel with *Madame Bovary* and *Sentimental Education*? What precisely was different about the structure of the force field at this time which made such a revolution in the genre of the novel possible? Martin Jay, in analysing the heuristic value of the force field concept to intellectual history, has put forward one solution to this problem. Discussing the genesis of the Frankfurt School in its formative period, he elucidates a number of elements specific to the social context of 1920s Frankfurt which interacted as 'a force field' of 'untotalised' and 'contesting impulses'. His point is that these forces resisted any form of harmonious integration into the whole. Therefore he notes: the non-traditional German university culture of Frankfurt, anti-mandarin with its rejection of intellectual specialism in favour of 'totalising knowledge'; the Institute for Social Research, the first Marxist organisation linked to a German university, critical of capitalism and dedicated to its overthrow; the urban milieu of the city of Frankfurt, which included innovatory developments in radio (committed to a public service broadcasting ethos), and newspapers and journalism concerned with cultural and social problems; and finally, the existence of a significant Jewish community with its distinctive, modernist culture. Institute members worked within all these contexts, moving easily between radio broadcasts, journalism, the university and left-wing political activism. Jay argues that the Institute enjoyed an 'eccentric' and 'marginal' relation with the formal university structure, the modernist urban culture and the radical political parties. Thus the Frankfurt School effectively emerged 'as the dynamic nodal point of all three, suspended in the middle of a socio-cultural force field without gravitating to any of its poles. Hostage to no particular defining context, it hovered in a kind of intellectual no-man's land' (Jay, 1993, p. 17).

Jay's analysis, while it veers towards contextual determinism, has the advantage of pointing to an open structure of overlapping and autonomous forces as defining elements in the genesis of a particular intellectual formation. His notion of context lacks the presence of a dominant centre, suggesting rather a pluralism which generates space for the new and original, a force field which enables new intellectual groups to emerge and exercise a distinctive role in the field of cultural production. Nevertheless, Jay's concept of force field approximates to a traditional idea of context, in which intellectual 'influences', broadly defined and existing independently of positions within a structure, function within homogeneous social space. There is no real sense of a hierarchically organised social structure, of its different levels and the links between them; nor any awareness of the subjective aspects of action, the values which dispose the different agents to engage in the varied practices of journalism, politics and academic labour. In short, Jay defines the force field through its intellectual currents and contents, by a downwards reductionism which tends to flatten the socio-cultural context.

In contrast, Frederick Jameson, in his studies of the postmodern as a new socio-cultural formation closely bound up with 'late capitalist' productive forces (for a fuller analysis see Chapter. 9), describes it as a force field dynamically integrated through the presence of a 'cultural dominant'. Jameson proposes a Marxist theorisation of force field, one in which an overarching aesthetic ideology governs the major forms of cultural practice, aesthetic realism for early capitalism, postmodernism for late capitalism. However, such a reductionism 'from above' has the effect of separating culture from social structure and simplifying the complex nature of social institutions, social relations and patterns of social action. Thus while the force field concept has redefined context in ways which open up the possibilities for cultural sociology to move beyond reductionist notions of sociological contextualism, by combining the historical with the objectively structural and the subjective, neither Jay nor Jameson succeeds in synthesising the objective (structural) with the subjective (reflexive). And while Bourdieu attempts an integration of the field with reflexivity and strives to avoid both upwards and downwards reductionism, he fails to account for the specifics of cultural change.

Limitations of Field Theory

Bourdieu has theorised culture in terms of production and reproduction, arguing against the short circuit effect in cultural sociology and linking culture with specific socio-historical contexts in which fields develop as social microcosms enjoying a relative autonomy and governed by a specific internal logic. Modern society is defined not in terms of a system but as a network of different, coexisting fields dependent on external factors for both their genesis and their struc-

104   *Cultural Theory and the Problem of Modernity*

ture (especially economic elements), but internally dynamic. Culture is thus realised through the relation of fields to habitus, to the values, strategies and actions of agents.

Bourdieu's is not the only cultural sociology that might be described as genetic structuralist, and it may be valuable to contrast briefly the field concept and the relevance of the short circuit effect to cognate ideas in the work of Karl Mannheim. One of the classic studies in this area is Mannheim's justly famous study of 'Conservative Thought' (1926) in which he proposed a homologous relation between the eighteenth-century Enlightenment philosophy of Kant and the political ideology of the French Revolution. Kant's philosophy expressed dynamic elements broadly similar to those espoused by the French revolutionaries. In contrast, German conservative thought reacted hostilely to the libertarian philosophy of the Enlightenment, seeking a conscious legitimation of the existing semi-feudal system against modern developments. Mannheim suggests that this romantic feudal reaction to liberalism (with its emphasis on organic evolution, historical continuity and traditional sovereignty) occurred because a weak capitalist class was dominated ideologically by a powerful, entrenched nobility. This 'style of thought' was thus nourished by social strata unaffected by modernity.

For Mannheim, distinctive social groups (bourgeoisie, proletariat and aristocracy) generate distinctive 'styles of thought' (or 'world views') which constitute a total, global perspective of an individual or epoch. Styles of thought correspond directly to the social position of a group or class in its struggle for power and the defence of its interests. As with Bourdieu, Mannheim argues that culture is imbricated in processes of social tension, competition, the desire for power and social recognition. There is thus a homologous relation between the intellectual field, the microcosm of intellectual thought, and macroclass structures. In Mannheim's analysis, agents exercise no active role: the genesis of a style of thought is the product of a 'collective subject', the social group (Mannheim, 1953, p. 198).

Mannheim's global analysis is based on a method which links the micro with the macro forces, an objectivist sociology which assimilates the former to the latter and effectively eliminates the ways structures are made and remade. In contrast, Bourdieu's concepts of field and habitus bring together the objective and the subjective dimensions, combining a focus on the historical genesis of structures, the collective basis of social action and practice, with the open nature of practice itself. Mannheim's cultural sociology fails to explicate the relation between the consciousness (values, aspirations and strategies) of a social group or class and the wider social context; the passage from one to the other is assumed to be unproblematic. But Mannheim's strength lies in his emphasis on the class or group form as a structural element of a context providing the collective basis for collective action. Here is one of the fundamental problems with Bourdieu's cultural sociology, for if field and habitus are both collective concepts, what is the difference between the notion of a class habitus and Mannheim's collective subject? Is this less a project of reflexive sociology than one of structural determinism? Many critics have pointed to the apparently deterministic nature of the concepts of field and habitus. Martin Jay has suggested that Bourdieu portrays individuals within a field as pulled around like lead particles in a magnetic field, although Bourdieu has explicitly rejected this analogy (Jay, 1993; Bourdieu and Wacquant, 1992, p. 97). Clearly there are determining elements involved in the workings of a field: structured around the distribution of capital, the internal logic of fields is linked with the type and volume of capital possessed by individuals and groups as they formulate strategies for advancing their positions. Such strategies include reconversion, for example, through which a group conserves its place in society by adapting and changing to new conditions and relations; thus business groups convert their economic capital into educational and cultural capital to secure their heirs' social standings.

Similarly, in his analysis of the French literary field after 1850 and the rise of a new form of literature (Flaubert's novels), Bourdieu argues that it was Flaubert's possession of a specific volume of cultural capital which enabled him to critique the established norms of bourgeois Parisian art and advocate a new and radical position, that of art for art's sake. It would have been impossible for groups and individuals lacking cultural capital to mount an effective challenge to the dominant principles of bourgeois aesthetic culture (Bourdieu, 1996).

At the same time, it is clear that within a field there exists a variety of possible practices; the consequences and effects of action taken in relation to others can never be adequately foreseen. Fields are sites of struggle and spaces of possibilities and while there is a deterministic element in Bourdieu's formulations, the field concept remains open to many potential results. In all social contexts individuals and groups have limited scope for action, for, as Marx noted, humanity does not choose the conditions under which it must act, but it is precisely such conditions which constitute the necessary basis enabling possible action to take place. Every situation is a complex mixture of determinism and voluntarism. As 'the locus of relations of force...and of struggles aimed at transforming it, and therefore of endless change', the field concept involves reflexive agents and specific modes of action. Although fields have similarities with systems, they are not systems; they are not the self-regulated and cohesive systems of functionalism but open-ended spaces of possible change.

Bourdieu's is a serious attempt to move towards a historical sociology of culture, one sharply at variance with orthodox Marxist sociological approaches. Both Parsons and the Frankfurt School, for example, overemphasise the structural and the synchronic over the genetic and historical, and fail to deal with the role played by collective agents in social and cultural change. As I have suggested, many of Bourdieu's formulations equally fail to account for the collective agent as an active element in the process of social transformation. But I believe Bourdieu has laid the basis for such a theory, one combining the objectivism of structuralism with the subjectivism of Sartre.

There are serious limitations, however. Bourdieu's weakness lies precisely in those areas of cultural sociology where the Frankfurt School are strongest: culture as immanent critique, as forms which oppose the closed, reified structures of modern society, opening a path to the possibility of an alternative world. For the Frankfurt School, culture was not so much a process of empowering individuals to act, as the embodiment of values which the existing society seeks to deny: culture as the 'otherness' of existing reality. For Bourdieu, the cultural is never 'otherness', but is tied closely to everyday practices, with the social and the political, woven with issues of power and judgements on taste. Culture is theorised as a process which reproduces symbolic power through *hysteris*, a 'misrecognition' which effectively supports and underpins the social order. While the sociocultural environment shapes, and is in turn shaped by human action and experience, culture can transcend these conditions only through its links with the past, the habitus. And while this is one of Bourdieu's most valuable ideas, it leaves unresolved the critical and partly autonomous role of culture itself as embracing universal and transcending values. This is the Marx problem I described in Chapter 1 – the transhistorical appeal of Homer's *Iliad* – which both Parsons and Gramsci resolved through the concepts of common culture and hegemony. Although Bourdieu's standpoint is closer to Gramsci than Parsons, it does raise quite different problems, especially those relating to the ways in which structures develop and change through collective action, as agents interact with others at different levels of society (or fields) and within specific institutions. In the next chapter I examine the problems of the autonomy of culture and the autonomisation of fields in relation to this notion of reflexive agent and to Bakhtin's concept of dialogism, interactionism (and the interaction order) and popular culture.

Chapter 7

Dialogism and Cultural Forms

Cultural Fields: Agency and Communication

In the previous chapters I have examined the broad trends in theorising culture, culminating in Bourdieu's attempted synthesis of the objectivist–subjectivist poles of cultural sociology. As we have seen, one of the major problems of both Marxist and sociological perspectives lay in analysing culture as a semi-autonomous sphere, or field, characterised by its own internal properties and forms, irreducible to the external conditions of social organisation. The functionalist tendency of Marxist and sociological analysis assumed coherence, unity and self-regulation of the social system (the macrostructures) which worked to integrate culture through a dominant centre (the world view of a social class, the common culture). Sociological functionalism, from Durkheim to Parsons, defined culture as a process in which individuals psychologically assimilate certain aspects of social structure, which then become institutionalised into the social system. This has the effect of weakening the analytic distinctions between meanings derived from culture and those from everyday social life. A close fit subsists between symbols, social behaviour and patterns of institutionalisation. The result is the marginalisation of the active role of the agent in the making of culture and a diminution of the creative and voluntaristic nature of action.

Weber's thesis of cultural differentiation, his interpretive sociology with its emphasis on the question of meaning and the motivation of agents, represents one solution, but the problem with Weber's formulations lies in their theoretical and empirical vagueness regarding the context of action, the precise socio-cultural physiognomy of agents and the modes of situating them within specific contexts. As we have seen, Bourdieu resolves this problem through the Durkheimian concept of mental structures which provide a bridge between subjectivism of habitus and objectivism of field. In this way Bourdieu advances an explanation of the genesis of fields and different forms of cultural production (situational specificity), and the complex ways agents contribute and relate to the structure and transformation of fields (internalist perspective). Unlike Weber, Bourdieu grounds the autonomy principle contextually in historical development and collective action.

However, Bourdieu's formulations generate a further set of problems. While defining habitus and agent in terms of their 'creative active and inventive capacities', Bourdieu identifies the dispositions as products of 'economic and social processes' which are more or less reducible to the particular 'external constraints' of the 'conditions of existence' (Bourdieu, 1990a, p. 50). The result is a one-dimensional concept of agent, one incapable of standing back and reflecting on values and meaning. In short, the theory of habitus suggests a limited and deterministic notion of agent and not a reflexive social self whose social and cultural identity arises out of complex interactions with others. Reflexivity belongs more to the field than to the agent. As fields achieve autonomy, with agents taking up new positions, they mobilise and invoke the history of the field within their own work: characters in Flaubert's novels, for example, refer to characters in Balzac, thus marking the access of the novel to a reflexivity that 'is one of the foremost manifestations of the autonomy of a field' (Bourdieu, 1996, p. 101).

Bourdieu, however, stresses that it is not a question of agents mechanically reproducing the structure of a field, but rather of the creative capacity of the habitus, which transcends the material conditions of existence. However, because Bourdieu has theorised fields as sites of struggles over scarce resources, the notion of 'interest' functions as a crucial element in determining the practices which aim at monopolisation and domination. It is not a question of agents consciously evaluating principles and fundamental beliefs in a critical and reflexive mode, but of action which is wholly instrumental. Agents follow specific practices which enable them to maintain or increase their assets, thus enhancing their social status – 'reproductive strategies' – or else practices which succeed in transforming one type of capital into another (economic capital into cultural or symbolic capital) – 'conversion strategies' – and thus advancing their claims to legitimacy.

Bourdieu's model focusses on a concept of agent based in selfishness and egoism, and concerned almost entirely with the pursuance of individual goals. Thus struggles over genres within the cultural field – modernist against realist novel, for example – are presented as part of a broader struggle for cultural legitimacy between dominant and emerging groups, who defend or redefine the nature of the genre for strategic purposes. Indeed, Bourdieu argues that the logic of practice always conforms to economic calculation, even when it might suggest 'disinterestedness'; the logic of fields effectively corresponds to the reproductive structures of capitalist economy, class struggles and ideology. The field of education, for example, reproduces capitalist class relations, generates a legitimating ideology and continually leads to the conversion of economic into cultural capital. A homologous relation is thus posited between the internal and external struggles, so that the education field (like the cultural field) embodies the conflicts and tensions between different social classes and fractions of classes (the 'field of power'). While not reflecting class relations directly, fields function as microcosms of class struggle and the logic of the capitalist market. Similarly, in describing select cultural institutions and salons – Bayreuth, Venice, Florence, etc. – as universes of social exclusivity 'in which everything is classified' and taste dependent on mastering such classifications, Bourdieu reduces culture to the basics of class relations (Bourdieu, 1990a, p. 137). There is no sense of agents choosing and evaluating art and literature other than in terms dictated by the social necessity of status distinction.

There is, then, a tendency to subtly elide the cultural and the social without giving sufficient weight to the former. Culture has its own history, in the same way that cultural forms – literary genres for example – enjoy a partly autonomous reality apart from the material specifics of production and social context. If the transformative capacity lies in the relation of agent (through the habitus) to field, a relation contingent on the field itself, then it still leaves open the question of the transformative capacity of the forms themselves and their complex relation to cultural history. If the concept of culture is confined solely to fields, and subfields, it loses its links with history and may lead to an inward-looking notion of culture, one sealed off from its own history and society.

It is true that Bourdieu argues that fields are the products of history, with their dynamic properties inherent internally, in the relations and struggles between different positions which are specifically situated in historical time. He fails, however, to deal with the problem of cultural time, with the fact that culture develops unevenly in its relation with other forces in society. He ignores, for example, the possibility that forms of popular culture developing during periods antedating the autonomisation of fields (which Bourdieu locates with capitalist modernity) may exercise an active role in the genesis and structure of modern cultural forms. (Examples here are the picaresque form of the novel, which survived from pre-modern culture to inform the structures of late eighteenth-and early nineteenth-century novels, and carnival elements derived from pre-modern popular festivities which shape the forms of contemporary satire – but see pp. 126–9 for further discussion.) Furthermore, the study of culture implies both its production and modes of reception in fields transformed by historical development, raising the problem of analysing the ways cultural forms become part of cultural history. This is not simply an argument about the transformation of genres and works over time, or that art works enjoy a future, any of which can be adequately accommodated to Bourdieu's model and is, in fact, integral to it. Rather, the question of reception is one not of cultural appropriation by specific classes, but of a universalising appropriation of past forms for their power in generating new meanings for the present and a sense of cultural identity. While such receptions are closely linked with cultural groups (in education, the media, the theatre and publishing), they are not reducible to narrowly defined interests. It is difficult to see, for example, how the variety of interpretations of English Renaissance drama during the past four centuries, with their references to cultural history and cultural identity, can be assimilated to an instrumentalist concept of action (Griswold, 1986).

The theory of fields clearly assumes a model of communicative action. Both Bourdieu and Williams emphasise the role of communication in culture, but it remains unclear how the communication process actually works in relation to agents. Bourdieu's relational model suggests limitations, in that the inter-subjective elements of social relations fail to enter the chain of communication. All action, for example, takes place through 'positionality', not interaction, for it is Bourdieu's argument that structures cannot be reduced to the interactions and practices through which they express themselves. Because they have certain properties, bound up with their positions within a field, agents are socially active and exercise effects, but only because of the objective position occupied. In this way Bourdieu conceives communicative action arising on the basis of positionality, so that cultural analysis avoids reducing objective structures to the subjective state of the agents generated through interaction. Social relations must not be reduced to those of communication. But without interaction there is no communication, no dialogue between those occupying different positions, no living exchange of ideas, judgements and aspirations, and no grasp of the ways in which agents actually change and develop their sense of cultural identity and notion of selfhood. How can reflexivity constitute an integral part of Bourdieu's project if the conditions which enable a reflexive response, creative and voluntarist action are theorised away? Because of the instrumentalist nature of action as Bourdieu conceives it, there is no room for the autonomy of ideas, values and critical thought, other than as means to achieve status and cultural domination.

Finally, the link between the micro and macro levels remains unclear, for while habitus explains the agent's strategic orientation to goals, the mental frameworks of habitus fail to account for the precise ways the agent's experience of structure (the field) is translated into cultural forms. How, in short, does the background become the foreground? What is the link between culture as social practice (external) and culture as specific aesthetic forms (internal)? If culture is narrowly defined in terms of fields and instrumental action then culture is reduced to the specifics of social context. But the creation of culture goes beyond the conditions of its production. Culture lives in great time. Cultural forms survive their origins, maintain a presence in different historical periods and societies through new modes of reception, and invigorate new cultural practices and artefacts. Bourdieu's sociology of culture, for all its strengths, fails to engage with the deep historical roots of culture and its immanent nature. As there is a deficit of subjectivism, voluntarism, reflexivity and no adequate theory of intersubjective communication, so Bourdieu's cultural sociology lacks an adequate concept of culture itself. In opposing the Frankfurt

School's affirmative theory of culture as opposition and utopia, of culture as alternative to the existing reality, Bourdieu leans increasingly towards an impoverished historical–sociological notion. In contrast, one of the most important contributions to the historical sociology of culture was first elaborated in the work of the Russian sociologist, Bakhtin, whose work brings together interaction, dialogue, active agents, a cultural sociology built around the making of culture and its dialectical and subversive nature.

Bakhtin: Culture, Self and Dialogue

The work of Mikhail Bakhtin has exerted and continues to exert an enormous influence in the field of contemporary cultural theory, although the reception of his major ideas since the 1970s has tended to focus on the literary and philosophical at the expense of the cultural. His contribution embraces studies of philosophical aesthetics, language, literary theory, the history of the novel and popular culture, and the history and philosophy of culture generally. In their biography of Bakhtin, Clark and Holquist (1984) make the point that the central thread of his whole work, first enunciated in *The Architectonics of Answerability* (1919–24), is the parallel between the building of texts and the building of the self. Bakhtin identified a necessary, organic relation between the social activity of agents as they sought to define and transform themselves and literary or cultural forms which are shaped in a similarly dynamic mode. Bakhtin expresses here the idea that the forces constituting a social context do not mechanically and externally exert an effect, but enter the self, texts and language, for example, as necessary constituting components. In short, Bakhtin raised the fundamental problem of how the background becomes the foreground so that, as he argued in his later study of Dostoevsky (1929), every literary work is internally, immanently sociological.

Although the term 'architectonics' drops out of Bakhtin's vocabulary to be replaced by 'structure' and/or 'construction', the basic principle remains central to his theory of culture. He defines architectonics as the ways different elements become integrated and consummated into distinctive wholes. Thus the social self and cultural forms building up from disparate elements, or parts, into a 'consummated whole' is the result of actual creative action and not of external impersonal forces. However, the attempts to form links between disparate materials always run the risk of losing the living and non-merging participants in events and hence those creative forces which generated the events themselves. What Bakhtin means here is that the 'consummation' of the whole, a self or a text for example, can never be total: there will always be an element of 'outsideness' involved. For example, as I become and realise myself as a 'self', I become aware of my relations with others in the very moment in which I transform myself through action. Without the 'other', the self could not exist; but this does not suggest a merging of its identity with the others or with the whole. Thus while the building of a self constitutes a process that implies integration and consummation (the unique self), the self, nevertheless, remains partly outside itself. And because there is no coincidence between the inner and outer self, life can never achieve a state of total consummation (Bakhtin, 1990, p. 122).

Bakhtin's concept of the self and wholeness is grounded firmly within the socio-cultural world as it exists. In contrast to the theories of Western Marxists such as Lukács and Adorno, Bakhtin has no sense of a deeply alienated social world which must be made whole again in a distant utopia. Bakhtin's social world is constructed by means of the here-and-now relation of self and other, and by the use of language through dialogue, for communication, development and change. Architectonics celebrates action, movement and energy, and identifies the defining principle of social life as the making of self and other through dialogue:

> For in order to live and act I need to be unconsummated, I need to be open to myself... I have to be, for myself, someone who is axiologically yet-to-be, someone who does not co-incide with his already existing makeup. (ibid., p. 13)

Although Bakhtin's is a philosophy not a sociology of action, these concepts play a decisive role in the later sociological studies. The *Architectonics* was clearly opposed to the prevailing Marxist-Leninist orthodoxy, which relegated the agent, the self, to a reflex of the economic and class structure, conceiving its relation with society in strictly mechanistic terms. For Bakhtin, the self–other relation was dialogic in that the self does not exist as a fixed, finished and finalised datum, but is in a state of constant activity. In his studies of the novel, popular culture and historical discourse, Bakhtin was concerned to show the dialogic (or polyphonic) nature of social life, with its basis in open-ended dialogue:

> To live means to participate in dialogue: to ask questions, to heed, to respond, to agree... In this dialogue a person participates wholly and throughout his whole life: with his eyes, lips, hands, soul, spirit, with his whole body and deeds. He invests his entire self in discourse, and this discourse enters into the dialogic fabric of human life. (Bakhtin, 1984, p. 293)

Bakhtin's distinction between dialogism and monologism is central to his theory of self: monologism conceives the other as finished, complete, an object of consciousness, while dialogism celebrates the unfolding, unfinished consciousness which lives only through its relations with others. Monologism leads to a turning inwards, an enclosing of the self, to separation and isolation; dialogism abhors enclosure, turning outwards to encounter and respond to the consciousness of others: 'I am conscious of myself and become myself only by revealing myself for another, through another, and with the help of another' (ibid., p. 287). Dialogism is thus grounded in alterity, 'To be means to communicate.' Bakhtin argues that this dialogic self is given its most profound literary expression in Dostoevsky's novels in which the hero constantly seeks to overturn the words of others which might 'externalise' and 'finalise' his sense of self. Bakhtin cites the hero of Dostoevsky's novella *Notes from Underground*, whose polemic against socialism 'is precisely the idea that man is not a final and defined quantity upon which firm calculations can be made; man is free and can, therefore, violate any regulating norms which might be thrust upon him' (ibid., p. 59).

Bakhtin's concept of self is profoundly reflexive, for everything which is experienced internally is turned outwards to encounter the words of others. In this way the self exists on the boundaries between its own and the other's consciousness, between its words and those of others. It is this which enables the self to reflect on its others and to respond actively, so that the other's words become part of oneself. As Bakhtin puts it, I need the other in order to 'author' myself.

As the self involves a tension between the dialogic and the monologic elements in social life, so culture itself is theorised as a struggle between two fundamental intellectual tendencies: first, those associated with centripetal forces, which seek to close off the social–cultural world by enclosing it within the idea of system (certain forms of philosophy, aesthetics, and sociology), a process which effectively impoverishes it; and, second, those linked with centrifugal forces, which strive to maintain openness by rejecting the idea of system and boundaries. To theorise culture is to celebrate richness, diversity, fluidity and borders. In the *Architectonics*, Bakhtin was concerned with establishing an appropriate methodology for the study of culture, arguing that any science which deals with cultural domains, or fields, must preserve all 'the complexity and fullness and distinctiveness of the object under study' while bringing to light its links with specific sociocultural contexts. The *Architectonics* is not, however, a sociology of culture: but its themes recur in Bakhtin's later sociological studies. His concept of culture is particularly significant in its break from the positivistic base–superstructure model with its assumption of culture constituting a specific space of materialised institutions, practices and meanings, all enclosed by well-defined boundaries. The whole of Bakhtin's thought opposed boundaries: he rejected the idea that culture has its own 'inner territory' which can be identified, categorised and finalised. For Bakhtin, culture is realised through differences within communities, the modes of interaction and attempts by individuals to overcome and go beyond the social and political mechanisms within society which aim to define and fix identity – as, for example, in some contemporary sociologies of culture which finalise the individual through membership of a 'youth culture', or 'high culture', or the culture of a particular occupation or profession or family. Bakhtin see sculture as an unfolding, incomplete process which lives on borders consisting of differences which find their unity through dialogue. His studies of popular culture (discussed on pp. 126–9) exemplify his concepts of self, other, culture and language as border phenomena. In his study of Rabelais, for example, he notes the mocking and satirical function of laughter in medieval popular culture, laughter which criticised offical culture (the state, religion), enabling ordinary individuals to exist as autonomous selves within a 'free and open' zone, their identity linked with the humour of the streets, taverns, market-place and square. The culture of laughter bordered high/low institutions, the dominant political and religious institutions and ideologies, and the institutions and practices of everyday popular culture.

Bakhtin's complex notion of border can be further illuminated by contrasting his semiotic concept of culture with that of the cultural anthropologist, Clifford Geertz, who also adopts a semiotic model. For Geertz, the task of cultural analysis lies in distilling the different levels of meaning which characterise specific cultural practices within definite communities. Culture engages with the symbolic order, with the communication of meanings. Thus cultural analysis takes the fragmentary and momentary elements of everyday practice, and trans- forms them into a fixed 'said' of social discourse, a finalised text, so to speak, of its culture. Hence in his most famous study, 'Deep Play: Notes on the Balinese Cockfight', Geertz interprets the cockfight as an art form communicating specific meanings to its participants. The analysis is external in that Geertz takes for granted that such meanings have already been established, and he does not raise ques- tions about the inner meaning of the events for the participants. Culture as a text, the 'said', is enclosed within a prescribed structure of rituals, symbols and practices existing through space and time (Geertz, 1973).

This external approach is what Bakhtin calls 'outsideness', compre- hending culture through the categories shaping its material reality, for cultures reveal themselves wholly and in depth only when viewed from the outside, generating a dialogue between them, between the present and the past. 'In the realm of culture, outsideness is a most powerful factor in understanding' (Bakhtin, 1986, p. 7). But this necessary methodological principle has the effect of finalising the nature of culture. Outsideness must, therefore, be complemented by analysis from the inside, from the unfolding and dynamic historical nature of culture itself which, existing on boundaries, resists such finalising methodology. In contrast to Geertz, Bakhtin proposes that in cultural analysis meanings are always in a process of being and becoming, always as dialogue, and cannot be established as given before analysis (Geertz, 1973).

Discourse, Language and Culture

Although the *Architectonics* laid the basis of his later studies of litera- ture and art, Bakhtin developed his distinctive sociological approach to culture out of a critical dialogue with the Russian formalists and Sausserian linguistics. The leading formalist scholars (Eichenbaum, Shklovsky, Tomashevsky and Tynyanov) were primarily literary and linguistic theorists, seeking to apply scientific methods to the analysis of literary forms and literary language, and the evolution of specific literary genres such as the epic, novel and forms of popular literature.

Describing their approach as an empirical 'independent science of literature' based on 'an objective consideration of the facts', the formalists defined themselves as 'specifiers', their methodology based on the literary text as an autonomous structure. The meaning of texts lay in their internal properties, in their 'literariness', that which makes a given work a work of literature (Erlich, 1981, pp. 171–3). The analysis of literature was conceived in purely synchronic terms, an emphasis derived from the structural linguistics of Saussure with its conception of language as an evolving system structured by internal regulative principles. Meaning was internal to the system, to the relation of words to each other, to difference and identity. Thus to understand the meaning of the word 'red' it becomes necessary to know what blue and green and so on are, what red is not, and as language constitutes a system of differences so the individual units have their identity through their relations with other units. Saussure frequently compared the system of language to the game or system of chess, in which the identity of each piece flowed from its differences with the other pieces; his main point – shared by the formalists – was that no utterance could be understood without reference to the system which governed its meaning, that is, to an underlying code which remained independent of social and historical change.

Saussure's anti-contextualism, his distinction between synchronic (elements coinciding in time without any reference to historical change) and diachronic (evolution, change) analysis, had the effect of reinforcing the antinomy between system and history which characterised formalism and its development into structuralism. Because language exists as a system of 'pure values which are determined by nothing except the momentary arrangement of its terms', synchronic analysis always exerts priority over the diachronic and historical. Language is thus 'a system of interdependent terms in which the value of each term results solely from the simultaneous presence of the others' (Saussure, 1974, p. 114). But while this mode of theorising is valuable for grasping cultural entities as relations and not things, it effectively eliminated the living interactions between cultural forms and their contexts. Although structuralism went beyond the formalists' preoccupation with literary language, to study the wider cultural system of which literature formed part, it failed both to show how the two systems were connected and how and why change takes place. The striking things about the later developments of structuralism (especially those in cultural theory) are the total disregard for sociological analysis and the failure to grasp cultural forms and processes as contextually historical phenomena. Reducing the variety and complexity of cultural forms to an underlying system of rules removes all questions of the making of culture and the interactions between the different levels of cultural practice and the resultant forms. As was noted with Bourdieu, structuralism seeks to 'enclose' and impose boundaries, to substitute formal patterns, sequences and regularities for the messy heterogeneity of living history.

Bakhtin accepted the Formalists' rejection of essentialist philosophical truths and universal concepts of literary form, but rejected their internalist perspective arguing that external social and historical forces exercised a constituting role in the genesis of aesthetic forms. It was not the case that literary genres such as the epic poem, adventure novel and biographical novel evolved independently of the historical context; and describing the development of genre in terms of an evolutionary law the Formalists failed to grasp and theorise the crucial role played by culture in this process.

The *Architectonics* had suggested that the key to understanding lay in dialogue, in the communicative relation of self to other. Although Saussure's linguistic theory had not given priority to the role of dialogue, Bakhtin shared his emphasis on the collective nature of language, 'a system of signs' governed by certain laws and structure. Describing 'a science that studies the life of signs within society' as semiology, Saussure argued 'that if we are to discover the true nature of language we must learn what it has in common with other semiological systems' such as 'rites and customs' and thus Saussure further distinguished between the syntagmatic and paradigmatic relations between signs: the syntagmatic relating to the position a sign occupies in an utterance so that the meaning of a word depends on its relations with other words in a sentence; while paradigmatic relates to words absent from the actual utterance but which could have been used through their similar grammatical functions, related meanings (synonyms and antonyms) and sound patterns (Saussure, 1974, pp. 16–17).

Bakhtin was more concerned with the syntagmatic features of language, the sentences of living speech rather than the more abstract paradigmatic level of the system of signs. And he went further than

Saussure by grounding the linguistic sign contextually arguing that the meaning of signs was diachronic and relational, involving modes of interaction between different speakers and their practical use of words within sentences.

Bakhtin distinguished two paradigms of language theory, which he called 'individualistic subjectivism', which located language within the individual consciousness, and 'abstract objectivism', which conceived language paradigmatically as a system of rules and relations existing independently from history, social context and individual speech. While acknowledging the clarity and rigour of Saussure's formulations, Bakhtin criticised the tendency to separate language from history by defining it as a system (*langue*) existing apart from the random, systemless nature of history itself. 'Formal, systematic thought about language is incompatible with living, historical understanding of language. From the system's point of view, history always seems a series of accidental transgressions' (Bakhtin and Volosinov, 1973, p. 78). Language exists only through historical time with its rich variety of context-bound speech acts or utterances (*parole*), its use constantly shifting from one context to another so that the word becomes effectively 'decentred', saturated with the intention and values of others. Language constantly evolves from one generation to another, involving individuals in a 'stream of verbal communication' (ibid., p. 81). 'Abstract objectivism' theorises language externally (synchronically) to this 'stream' (diachrony), failing to make adequate linkages between the actual living words and the abstract system itself.

For Bakhtin, language was thus inseparable from its specific socio-historical context and fundamental role in communication:

> Language acquires life and historically evolves...in concrete verbal communication, and not in the abstract linguistic system of language forms, not in the individual psyche of speakers. (Medvedev and Bakhtin, 1978, p. 129)

Because any word depends on its context for meaning, it follows that the constitutive nature of that word itself embodies a multiplicity of meanings:

> meaning belongs to a word in its positions between speakers...realised only in the process of active, responsive understanding. Meaning does not reside in the word...[but] in the effect of interaction between speaker and listener (Bakhtin and Volosinov, 1973, p. 95).

But Saussure's separation of utterance (parole) from language (langue) conceived language as something passively assimilated by individuals and not as a 'function of the speaker'. Saussure failed to examine dialogic relations in the linguistic interaction of different speakers. Bakhtin overcame this dualism between a binary opposition of a 'pure' language and an 'impure', historically specific utterance, by defining the word as dialogic: 'Language is alive only in the dialogic intercourse of those who make use of it. Dialogic intercourse is the genuine sphere of the life of language [which] is permeated by dialogic relationships' (ibid., pp. 102–3). Language as discourse is active and productive, involving social evaluations of the present, the past and the possibilities inherent in the future. Semantic and logical relations of language lack the dialogic aspect until they become utterances and embody the positions of different speakers. Thus discourse links individuals in a chain of communication:

> Utterances are not indifferent to one another, and are not self-sufficient; they are aware of and mutually reflect one another. Each utterance is filled with echoes and reverberations of other utterances to which it is related by the communality of the sphere of speech communication...Each utterance refutes, affirms, supplements and relies on others...and somehow takes them into account. (Bakhtin, 1986, p. 91)

For Saussure, language formed an already existing abstract and stable system which effectively eliminated the impress of historical time, while for Bakhtin language inhered only within living speech, the creative capacities of speaking itself. Through speech, agents transform both the social context in which speech occurs and themselves. As Morson notes, this represents one of Bakhtin's most radical ideas: who speaks creates (Morson, 1986, p. 67). Individuals do not receive language ready-made, to be handed down and passively accepted, but actively and imaginatively use it to express and exchange ideas and engage in ideological interaction. Bakhtin emphasises that ideological pheonomena exist materially as signs:

> The reality of ideological pheonomena is the objective reality of social signs. The laws of this reality are the laws of semiotic communication and are directly determined by the total aggregage of social and economic laws. Ideological reality is the immediate superstructure over the economic basis. Individual consciousness is not the architect of the ideological

superstructure, but only a tenant lodging in the social edifice of ideological signs. (Bakhtin and Volosinov, 1973, p. 13)

Thus ideology is theorised not as a finished, totalising structure, a coherent world view (as it was in orthodox Marxism) embedded in human consciousness, or literary or philosophic texts, but as a living process of social interaction between individuals. For Bakhtin, ideological phenomena penetrate deeply to the sources of social life in the words, gestures and sounds of the material world.

Although couched in Marxist terms, *Marxism and the Philosophy of Language* was highly critical of the tendency of Soviet Marxism to assimilate ideologies mechanistically to social context and conceptualise the superstructure in passive terms. Similarly, Saussurian linguistics also failed to account for ideology in its analysis of the relation of individual to society as a natural rather than a social phenomenon. The social role of ideology played no role in the development and usages of language. Thus the social character of the categories employed in linguistic analysis was largely ignored, leading Saussure to separate discourse from both the agent and the culture.

Discourse forms the central point in Bakhtin's analysis of culture, an active, productive practice involving value judgements of the historical present, past and future. Traditionally linguistics had defined its object of study as dead, written language, the isolated finished monological utterance divorced from its socio-cultural and verbal context. Such a standpoint eliminated all notions of active response to signs, or of understanding them. Active modes of communicative practice imply a dialogic perspective, and in Bakhtin's theory of language the dialogic nature of the utterance always involves an unfinalised, open relation of self to other in which the self, through its practical acquisition of languages, of speech genres (highly flexible, diverse, everyday modes of conversation, for example) becomes the sum of its discursive actions. All discourse implies simultaneous understanding between the speaker who listens and the listener who speaks:

> *Any true understanding is dialogic in nature.* Understanding is to utterance as one line of dialogue is to the next...meaning belongs to a word in its position between speakers...realised only in the process of active, responsive understanding... Meaning is the effect of interaction between speaker and listener produced via the material of a particular sound complex. (Bakhtin and Volosinov, 1973, pp. 102–3, emphasis in original)

Thus like Bourdieu, Bakhtin is arguing that speech communities are built around the positions of agents within a discursive field. The book on language had focused on speech genres, or speech forms (the subject of one of Bakhtin's final essays), defining the analysis of these as one of 'the most urgent tasks of Marxism'. All social groups have a repertoire of speech forms which are essential for 'ideological communication', forms determined by relations of production and 'the socio-political order'. While these formulations are glossed in Marxist terms, Bakhtin moves away from mechanism by arguing that while individuals conceive reality through language it is the speech genres which constitute the means of representing the social world in a structured, not chaotic form. Reality can be comprehended only through such means of representing it. Discourse, in short, does not merely reflect but organises and transforms its social context.

In notes written during 1970–1, Bakhtin reiterated this activist notion of language: 'Semiotics deals primarily with the transmission of ready-made communication using a ready-made code. But in live speech... communication is first created in the process of transmission, and there is, in essence, no code' (Bakhtin, 1986, p. 147). Thus language, because it lives only through the relations between speakers, and functions collectively through distinctive speech genres, is imbricated in struggle: language is the means whereby different social groups represent ideological values and affirm their cultural, political and social aspirations in relation to others. The historical development of language is not, as Saussure argued, one of harmonious evolution. The basic unit of speech, the utterance, is 'born, lives and dies' through the interpersonal relations of social interaction, and it is the form and character of the interaction which gives meaning to the utterance. The word is a social event: the expression and product of speakers and listeners. Verbal interchange is never homogeneous, or random, but hierarchically organised, and all utterances involve 'an intense interaction and struggle' between one's own and another's world, a process of opposing and interanimating each other. The utterance, then, is not simply the vehicle for individual expression but is multi-voiced, multi-accentual in that it always takes account of other voices in an open, fluid interaction. So discourse is theorised objectively and contextually as the arena of struggle between opposing voices (Bakhtin and Volosinov, 1973, p. 17).

Bakhtin's theory of dialogism is thus built around the notion of alterity, that the autonomy and individuality of the social self springs out of its necessary relation with the 'other' through open-ended dialogue. The social production of the self involves action, and 'performance', individuality as the product of open-ended practices. As Bakhtin put it, the self is 'the gift of the other' constituted in and through discourse as productive practice. Through dialogue, individuals gain knowledge, understanding and consciousness, because speech never belongs to one individual but is always involved in active relations with others.

As we have seen, Bakhtin rejected Saussure's distinction between speech as active, and listening as passive, arguing that 'the listener who understands passively does not correspond to any real participant in speech communication' (Bakhtin, 1986, pp. 69–70). Language lives through the utterance, through the everyday dialogic interaction between speakers and *discourse is oriented toward the person addressed*, oriented toward what that person it' (Bakhtin and Volosinov, 1973, p. 101, emphasis in original).

Bakhtin applied these ideas on language and discourse in the essays he wrote during the 1930s which explored the complex relation between European culture and languages and specific aesthetic forms, notably the novel. The theory of discourse outlined in these texts (published in English as *The Dialogic Imagination*) is strongly antipositivist, and Bakhtin echoes Max Weber's distinction between the methodology and epistemology of the human and natural sciences. Only the cultural sciences, he argues, acknowledge discourse as a proper subject in its own right. The methodology appropriate to the natural sciences deals with reified objects, which excludes the problem of engaging with, transmitting and interpreting the discourse of others. While sharing Weber's emphasis on understanding as the cornerstone of cultural sociology, Bakhtin conceived understanding as more than taking account of the other's actions contextually, but contextualising the other as a responsive, autonomous agent whose actions flow through a process of dialogic interaction. While language is a social cement that binds individuals into distinctive social groups, 'living discourse', with its assumption of at least two speaking subjects, is always dialogic. All discourse – conversation, religion, law, politics – presupposes a communicative relation between socially constituted individuals. And while a diversity of discourses and discursive strata coexist within a national language and culture, they do so not as isolated voices laid out in distinctive and separate culture enclaves, but as communities listening and speaking to one another. Bakhtin calls this 'heteroglossia', the diversity of everyday languages ('hetero- phony' is the diversity of individual voices) and one of his key points is that language remains alive, developing and dynamic through this internal pluralism.

He describes an ongoing struggle between the forces of heteroglos- sia (centrifugal) and those of centralisation and unification (centri- petal) in which the latter seek to establish authoritative artistic and ideological norms over the creation of a universal language and dominant cultural centre. This unitary language

> constitutes the theoretical expression of the historical processes of linguis- tic unification and centralisation...forces that struggle to overcome the heteroglossia of language, forces that unite and centralise verbal–ideologi- cal thought...which develop in vital connection with the processes of sociopolitical and cultural centralisation.

Bakhtin stresses that these centripetal forces are rarely so dominant that they can exclude the reality of heteroglossia completely. Within all cultures new, differentiated social groups arise 'in an intense and vital interaction with other social groups', and confronted by the diversity of other cultures and languages, the national culture can lose its hermetic character, with the goal of a single unitary language supplanted by a 'decentring' of the verbal–ideological world (Bakhtin, 1981, p. 368).

Bakhtin paints this process in broad brushstrokes, with a minimum of historical sociology. For the most part he deals in broad general- ities:

> Alongside the centripetal forces, the centrifugal forces of language carry on their uninterrupted work; alongside the verbal–ideological centralisa- tion and unification, the uninterrupted processes of decentralisation and disunification can go forward. (Bakhtin, 1981, pp. 271–2)

Within this general framework Bakhtin distinguished two forms of culture: the 'official' culture of the dominant social groups – hierarch- ical, closed and monologic; and the 'unofficial' culture of the 'people' – based in the heteroglossia of language and the realities of the everyday world, authentically human, open and exceeding its own boundaries. Popular and official culture are locked in struggle as the representatives of the latter seek to impose norms on the whole of society, especially within the religious, legal and literary texts. By elevating norms and canons above life itself, the official culture increasingly consists of 'dead, finished' elements. A cultural apparatus emerges (political, religious, literary and legal) charged with disseminating the dominant culture 'from above', thus marginalising and closing down other, alternative forms of discourse. In his substantive studies of Dostoevsky and Rabelais, Bakhtin attempted to trace the influence of the heteroglossia of popular culture on the genesis of the so-called high genres of European culture. Bakhtin was particularly concerned with the elements of the carnivalesque in this process, the ways unofficial culture becomes transformed into the foreground, 'low' culture invading the 'high'.

Unofficial Culture: The Concept of the Carnivalesque

As an archaic element in the process of cultural continuity, carnival has its origins in pre-industrial folk culture, and although its forms vary historically it constitutes an ever present universal element in human culture. In opposition to the monologic tradition of official culture, with its panoply of ecclesiastical and political cults and ceremonies, carnival embodied an alternative reality:

> A boundless world of humorous forms and manifestations opposed the official and serious tone...of feudal culture. In spite of their variety, folk festivities of the carnival type, the comic rites and cults, the clowns and fools, giants, dwarfs and jugglers, the vast and manifold literature of parody – all...belong to one culture of folk carnival humour. (Bakhtin, 1968, p. 4)

Carnival functioned to liberate humanity from the established order; it represented 'the suspension of all hierarchical rank, privilege, norms and prohibitions...hostile to all that was immortalised and completed'. The unofficial popular culture emphasised equality of human relationships, defining humanity in dynamic, not fixed, terms. Folk laughter is identified as the laughter of the whole community, simultaneously mocking, triumphant, derisory, assertive, denying, burying and reviving. As part of the carnival crowd the individual is aware 'of being a member of a continually growing and renewed people' in which folk laughter represents an element of victory 'over supernatural laws...the sacred...death', over everything oppressive and restrictive.

Carnival constituted a collective social institution giving rise to a specific literary form – the carnivalesque – expressed in the popular images crowding Rabelais's novel *Gargantua and Pantagruel*. Bakhtin terms this form 'grotesque realism' because of its excessive concentration on the material reality of the human body and its joyful celebration of eating, drinking, copulating and defecating. The grotesque image 'ignores the closed, smooth and impenetrable surface of the body and retains only its excrescences (sprouts, buds) and orifices, only that which leads beyond the body's limited space or into the body's depths' (Bakhtin, 1968, pp. 317–8). In his *Rabelais and his World* (1940), Bakhtin argued that writers such as Boccaccio, Cervantes, Shakespeare and Rabelais developed their artistic techniques and vision historically from the depths of a folk culture which, 'shaped during many centuries...had defended the people's creativity in non-official forms, in verbal expression or spectacle'. Bakhtin shows in rich detail the ways in which the background of the carnival becomes the foreground of grotesque realism:

> Thanks to this process popular-festival images become a powerful means of grasping reality; they served as a basis for an authentic and deep realism. Popular imagery did not reflect the naturalistic, fleeting, meaningless and scattered aspect of reality but the very process of becoming its meaning and direction. (Bakhtin, 1968, p. 72)

The carnivalesque is effectively a utopianism of absolute equality and freedom, the suspension of all social hierarchies and social distance, a time when the utopian truth becomes 'a real existing force' (ibid., pp. 264–5). In Bakhtin's formulations the symbolic and the social have been turned upside down as carnivalised forms subvert and transgress the official symbolic order. Traditional symbolic categories of the polite order are overthrown: grotesque images of the body, for example, supplant more decorous notions. It is not the destinies of individuals which are at stake in carnival, but the collective pranks, obscenities, coarse familiarity, a lack of seriousness, mock disputes all form the central philosophy of carnival with its ceremonies and images linked with crowning–triumph, uncrowning–mockery. The result is a deeply ambivalent outlook. For none of the carnivalised forces are complete, finished; there is no sense of a stable, integrated world, only one of restless movement from one state to another. As exemplar of carnival ambiguity, the 'mask' expresses all the mysteries of identity

> connected with the joy of change and reincarnation, with joyful relativity and the happy negation of uniformity and similarity; it rejects conformity to one's own self. The mask is related to transition, metamorphoses, the violation of natural boundaries. (ibid., pp. 39–40)

Throughout his detailed analysis of Rabelais's novel, Bakhtin stresses that the carnivalesque imagery is no straightforward reflection of an ephemeral, fragmentary and meaningless aspect of reality, but embodies a complex process of change full of human meaning, universality, optimism and direction. Carnivalesque forms communicate 'a profound historical awareness and deep understanding of reality' (ibid., p. 208). They celebrate openness and the capacity for self-renewal, liberating the individual from all forms of dogmatism and fanaticism. As he writes in his book on Dostoevsky, carnivalisation made possible 'the open structure of the great dialogue, and permitted social interaction between people to be carried over into the higher sphere of the spirit and the intellect'; the carnival sense of the world is expressed in the dialogic notion that no one can manage without another consciousness and'can never find complete fullness in himself alone' (Bakhtin, 1984, p. 177).

The dialogic, utopian and liberating nature of carnival has, however, been widely criticised, Bakhtin being accused of excessive idealism and historical inaccuracy. Carnival culture was far more ambivalent than Bakhtin's model suggests: ethnic groups, religious minorities and women were frequently demonised and abused, and rather than undermining official authority, carnivals were sanctioned and licensed by the dominant social classes, reinforcing existing social hierarchies through mechanisms of controlled protest. Licensed seventeenth-century Dutch carnivals avoided criticising Calvinist bourgeois culture; English carnivals, while inverting social relations, effectively reaffirmed monarchical authority by the ritual crowning of king and queen (Stalleybrass and White, 1986, pp. 13–19). Carnivals were also the sites of violent social conflict, even massacre (Le Roy Ladurie, 1981), functioning also as vehicles for economic development through assimilating foreign merchants and invigorating local markets. But such criticisms focus on the historical evolution of carnivals from their origins in the culture of the middle ages – Bakhtin's historical model – and their entwinement in modern economic and political institutions. Bakhtin makes the point that carnival loses its original, subversive and utopian dynamism through the development of capitalism and bureaucracy and the increasing rationalisation of culture, its forms impoverished and narrowed into modes of ritual and popular amusement, such as court masquerades, salons and popular, sentimental spectacle exemplified in English seaside fairs.

Although the historical rationalisation of carnival increasingly separates it from the life of the community, what is 'striking and original' about Bakhtin's concept of the carnivalesque, Stuart Hall has argued, 'is that it is *not* simply a metaphor of inversion, setting the "low" in the place of the "high", while preserving the binary structure of the division between them' for the low 'invades the high, blurring the hierarchical imposition of order; creating not simply the triumph of one aesthetic over another, but those impure and hybrid forms of the "grotesque"''. Culture is inextricably mixed, ambivalent, 'the reversability of cultural forms, symbols, language and meaning' challenging all hierarchical principles of 'cultural closure' (Hall, 1996, pp. 291–2). And although it degenerated into ossifying rituals, carnival maintained an active presence in modern European culture. Maynard Solomon has documented Mozart's passion for carnival and its fundamental role in his life and music. The carnivalesque elements of mockery, ridicule, burlesque, obsessive sexual wordplay, and double meaning are all expressed in Mozart's 'obscene riddles', his enthusiasm for the bawdy, the profane and bodily pleasures. 'Mozart's bawdy is a strategy of carnivalesque uncrowning, a humourous debasement of hegemony and hierarchy, of power and pomp, a parody of rationality, cleanliness and order' (Solomon, 1995, p. 359).

Thus while carnival is diminished, the carnivalesque survives: Bakhtin suggests that while originating in popular culture and its genres, the carnivalesque and the dialogic enter the genres of its culture, notably the novel, and while less significant for everyday cultural life, they become powerful structuring principles within aesthetic forms. Indeed, the novel becomes the focal point for Bakhtin's cultural theory.

Dialogism, Enclosure and Historical Context: The Case of the Novel

As the most significant literary genre of modern society, the novel belongs both to a specific historical context and to universal cultural tendencies, its many forms closely linked with the evolution of language and popular, unofficial culture. It is language which lays the foundation for the novel's development, and Bakhtin theorises the novel not for the possible ways it might reflect society but rather for its active shaping presence within the heteroglossia of culture.

Two issues dominate Bakhtin's account of the novel:

1. The relation of the novel to everyday language and discourse (to heteroglossia and heterophony), its many forms shaped by open dialogue or closed monologue – the problem of the diversity of voices as formal constituents of the polyphonic form of the novel.
2. The relation of the novel to deeper currents of culture, to existing forms already 'laden with meaning' within the popular traditions.

Bakhtin identifies the novel as the only literary genre that can grasp the basic principle of cultural life, its dynamic, unfolding nature, what he calls the 'spontaneity' of the 'inconclusive present'. At the heart of Bakhtin's sociology of culture is the idea of a decentred social–historical world, inconclusive, fluid and developing, in which there is no single overarching meaning but a diversity of meanings, just as there is a diversity of languages and voices.

In contrast, the epic depicts a finished rather than an open-ended reality, one in which the individual characters have already been formed, their values and actions wholly circumscribed by a social world that is bounded, complete and dominated by a static notion of the present. Unlike the epic, the novel has no unitary world view, rather it seeks to dramatise the inherent heteroglossia of language and the sense of the present as history. The novelist is drawn to everything uncompleted, with novelistic discourse depicting the present as 'life without beginning or end'. The indeterminate nature of the epic secures 'finalising structures' in which the social–historical world is rendered whole and finished. Epic discourse provides no chink through which the future might be glimpsed, for no further development is possible; novelistic discourse, in contrast, enjoys a direct link with developing historical reality. As an 'everquesting' genre, developing and dynamic, the novel is fundamentally non-canonical, existing on the borders with other genres (the novel, unlike other literary genres, absorbs other forms) and with its own culture: Rabelais's novel, for example, assimilated the popular festive forms of the carnival, everyday speech and the literary genre of the satire. The novel establishes 'maximal contact' with the potential inherent in the historical present, and can never be enclosed within its own form or a specific context.

Unlike traditional sociologies of the novel – Lukács's *Studies of European Realism*, Ian Watt's *The Rise of the Novel* – Bakhtin's rejects the theory of correspondences which assert a causal relation between the emergence of the novel and the structure of bourgeois society – new economic forms and classes, a distinctive middle-class reading public, circulating libraries and advances in printing technology. For Bakhtin, the novel is linked with the decomposition of the stable, verbal and ideological centralisation characteristic of periods of rapid social change when old, unified societies begin breaking up – he cites the Rennaissance as the exemplary instance – and the centrifugal forces of modernity weaken centralised authority. The novel both expresses and reproduces the multitude of languages, different discourses and cultures as they interact dialogically with one another. In contrast, the epic reproduces a sacred tradition of a national heroic past; the novel, exulting in diversity and pluralism, challenges all such notions of fixed boundaries (Bakhtin, 1981, pp. 21–31).

Although Bakhtin's theory of the novel at times comes close to Lukács's Marxist analysis – the novel as the dramatisation of the historical reality and movements of modern bourgeois society, representing the struggles between social classes, groups and individuals both objectively and subjectively (Lukács emphasises the 'interiority' of characters, their freedom, autonomy and possible sources of action) – he rejects Lukács's Hegelian reading of the history of the novel as an epic of the modern bourgeois world which seeks to unite the individual in an ideal world. Lukács's cultural Marxism is built on the fundamental dualism between a modern society becoming dehumanised and fragmented by its division of labour, and an ideal society of a pre-modern, vanished, integrated world. Bakhtin repudiates such ahistorical essences, utopias and teleological interpretations which tie the historical fate of the novel to that of a social class or culture.

What is so distinctive about Bakhtin's theory of the novel is its concern with the internal, specific formal properties which have their own autonomy and reality. Hence his emphasis on the concept of 'novelness', the anti-generic tendency of the novel to absorb all genres in its quest for the means of representing contemporary reality. He identifies two traditions of the novel form, the dialogic or polyphonic and the monologic or closed. The dialogic constitutes a distinctive new genre in European culture, existing in a dynamic relation with other genres and texts as well as undermining and subverting the norms and canons of the official culture. The earliest literary genres of epic, tragedy and lyric failed to deal adequately with the dialogism of everyday life, but unlike these genres the novel assimilates and organises elements such as time and space to create images of humanity that go against the grain of official culture. The ways space and time are organised Bakhtin calls the 'chronotope'. As an example, he notes how the public square constitutes either an 'elevated' category in literature, a 'state apparatus' which functions to reveal the state's authority over its citizens, or in more popular fiction it comprises the space of the common people with its bazaars, taverns and carnival institutions. In Balzac's novels, time and space are organised to undermine official culture in the depiction of salons and parlours as agencies of financial intrigue and corruption, the intersection of high politics and high finance. In this chronotope Balzac expressed the emerging new social relations of the July Monarchy (ibid., pp. 132, 246–7).

Official culture has the effect of enclosing great art works in its own time, cutting them off from the flow of open-ended history. For Bakhtin, great art lives in both the present and the future, breaking through the boundaries of its own period to live in other centuries more intensely and richer than in its own. This is the problem of enclosure, of theorising culture as a bounded, self-sufficient world. The chronotope suggests a dynamic, unfolding historical sense, one enclosed neither in its own time (the time of cultural creation) nor later as the subversive, radical elements find different receptions in different societies, publics and cultures.

For Bakhtin, culture is created through human action in which the dialogic element breaks down the sense of borders. The utterance, for example, exists on the border between speakers, between the said and the unsaid; and the utterance is always an answer to another utterance that has preceded it (Holquist, 1990, pp. 60–1). Culture abhors borders: it cannot be built from inert, reified, finished elements. Bakhtin's analysis of the novel focusses precisely on its potential for open and unfinalised dialogue. Thus it is not a question of linking the novel with a distinctive field, in a short circuit effect via class or economic forces. For like Bourdieu, Bakhtin rejects the external approach of social origins and biography for failing to grasp the 'essential...the genesis and structure of the specific social space in which the "creative project" was formed', the field of cultural producers or unofficial culture' (Bourdieu, 1993a, pp. 142–3; 1996, p. 83). Bourdieu, however, goes further, by analysing the institutional features of the cultural field, the 'space of producers' emphasising the role played by publishing houses, literary reviews and journals, the existing hierarchy of genres as the embodiment of official culture. In Bourdieu's analysis there exist two homologous structures – the works themselves (genres, themes) and the literary field as a field of forces and struggles which aim to transform the established relations of forces through a revolt against the cultural establishment and its canonised genres.

The autonomy of fields (with their internal specific laws, and relations of force between different positions), their increasing independence from external history, suggests that cultural developments flow from the immanent elements of the field itself. Bourdieu's model encloses the notion of culture and its artefacts firmly within distinctive boundaries, and he defends the autonomisation process as one way of linking aesthetic works with society while avoiding the short circuit effect. But this approach has the effect of severing art works from the broader historical culture – not simply from 'great time' (a difficult sociological concept), but from a historically contextualised notion of reception. Bourdieu conceives cultural creation from the point of view of the market, which always exercises a determinate role in the genesis, volume and distribution of economic and cultural capital. Thus the literary field is no vague background or milieu, but a structure which obeys specific laws relating to particular forms of capital. In his analysis of the French literary field in the second half of the nineteenth century, Bourdieu describes the important role played by Flaubert in its development. Flaubert's access to cultural capital allowed him to situate himself between two dominant poles of the field, between social realism and art for art's sake, and create a new kind of novel and literature. Flaubert was thus able to reverse the basic economic principles at work within the market and generate a universe of belief built around the values of disinterestedness and artistic value. Bourdieu effectively narrows and impoverishes his concept of cultural field by reducing it to either a positive response to market economic forces (as with commercialised art and literature) or a negative response facilitated by ownership of cultural capital.

Bakhtin's dialogism offers a way out of this reduction. I have suggested that Bourdieu's cultural sociology is potentially of great value, and it would be wrong to dismiss it for its functionalist and/or structuralist residues. His concept of habitus, for example, involves both subjective and objective structures: subjectively the agent, or self, has dispositions which, when realised within the objective framework of a field, produce new positions and new relations. Flaubert, for example, through his habitus generated a radical new position by creating a new literature, a new concept of author and a new genre of the novel. The relation between the subjective and the objective succeeds in changing the relations between all positions within the field. But as I have noted earlier, Bourdieu's concept of the agent or self remains problematic, lacking the quality of reflexivity which dialogism necessitates. Bourdieu's model of cultural production is loaded against the autonomy of the agent, setting strict limits to the degree of self awareness, relations with others and critical consciousness. What is missing is the means of understanding: how does the agent grasp his or her sense of identity in relation both to self and other? Understanding implies that the agent succeeds in situating him or herself outside events to reflect on their meaning and possibilities for both self and other. But for Bourdieu the other seems to play no role in the construction of self, with everything coming from within the habitus and its relation with the field. There is no sense of a dialogic interaction between self and others and field: the other merely occupies a specific position which stands as a barrier to the successful realisation of the self's dispositions.

There is, too, the problem of the architectonics of fields. How is it possible to build a field without the active involvement of a constructive, reflexive mind? To be part of a field assumes an understanding both of the whole and one's place within it as an unfinished and developing project or event, and simultaneously a consciousness of the whole field seen from the outside as a structure existing in space and time, as fixed and complete. It is this architectonic activity which enables the self to grasp the wholeness of a field, but Bourdieu's cultural field exists only as a fully materialised form, existing within well-defined boundaries. In contrast, Bakhtin conceives culture in terms of borders which lack a sovereign internal territory and dominant voices: a cultural field lives through the dialogic interaction between agents, many voices and meanings.

Dialogism thus presents an entirely new angle to the concept of force field, one which emphasises the interplay between the internal and unfinalised and the external and finished, a double movement necessary in any adequate cultural analysis. To enclose in the manner of Bourdieu (as well as structuralist and positivistic sociologies) leads ultimately to a closing down of dialogue and the imposition of a narrow and impoverished notion of culture. Culture is characterised by a historical logic indifferent to Bourdieu's logic of cultural competition: as new cultural forms are created out of the depths of popular culture they become transformed through great time and a long duration, renewed and reinterpreted by an ongoing dialogue between past and present culture. No modern culture, or society, lives separated from its past: for, as Marx, Gramsci, Parsons and Bakhtin have argued, culture is never merely the product of its specific context. As Bakhtin wrote at the end of his life:

> There is neither a first nor a last word and there are no limits to the dialogic context (it extends into the boundless past and the boundless future). Even *past* meanings, that is, those born in the dialogue of past centuries, can never be stable (finalised, ended once and for all) – they will always change (be renewed) in the process of subsequent future development of the dialogue. (Bakhtin, 1986, p. 170)

Bakhtin's fundamental concepts of the carnivalesque and hybridisation of culture, alive through plural voices and many meanings, his critique of monologism and dominant meaning, clearly suggest a theory of modernity. Similarly, Bourdieu's concept of the autonomisation of fields develops Weber's thesis of rationality specifically as a theory of modernity. The next chapter explores the problems posed to cultural theory by the contemporary concern with the concept and theory of modernity.

Chapter 8

Modernity and Culture

What is Modernity?

In earlier chapters I outlined the development of the concept of culture in Marxism and sociology, paying particular attention to the contributions of Gramsci and Weber with their critiques of reductionism and their emphasis on human action and purpose. The discovery of culture as an autonomous realm of human values, action and structure corresponds closely with the emergence of an advanced industrial capitalism with powerful modernising forces that generated a fluid and pluralist social structure, new social classes and fractions of classes, new professions, new industries and services, and populations increasingly concentrated in burgeoning urban centres. And it was during the second half of the nineteenth century that the arts, too, were modernised: art, literature, music (as well as philosophy and psychology) were transformed through the development of new modes of narrative and concepts of time (for example, the stream of consciousness novel); painting and music broke from the traditional mimetic forms to conceive a fleeting and fluid reality with no apparent centre (impressionism in painting, Debussy, Schoenberg, Webern and Berg in music); while the expressionist theatre of Strindberg and Wedekind abandoned all notions of a stable and unified self.

The modernist movement in the arts attests to the broad changes taking place within the aesthetic sphere, the search for a new language and new forms to provide expression to the 'newness' of modern society. It would be wrong, however, to regard modernism as a unified movement: there was no single modernism, but many modernisms,

136

some of them hostile to modernity while others embraced enthusiastically the 'new'. In painting, for example, the surrealists identified modernity with scientific rationalism, positivism, utilitarianism and the affirmation of a dehumanised machine culture, while the Italian futurists gloried in the new technology, 'the world's magnificence' enriched by 'the beauty of speed' and 'the vibrant nightly fervour of arsenals and shipyards blazing with violent electric moons...' (Marinetti, 1996). And while the modernist architecture of Le Corbusier and the Bauhaus embraced the new scientific ethos, British literary modernism (Conrad, James, Yeats and Eliot) distanced itself from this new world, and through poetic language and complex aesthetic forms, elevated itself above the everyday world of popular, commercialised culture, defining itself as autonomous and critical of the new cultural consumerism of newspapers, magazines, popular fiction and music-halls. The 'aesthetically new' confronted the mass-produced new by arrogating a distinct autonomous realm above and apart from modern mass society.

Modernism is thus the aesthetic logic of a modernising society, an aesthetic movement built on the principles of differentiation and autonomy. Modernist art forms were anti-mimetic and anti-representational, generating and not reflecting reality, reflexively engaged in a critical dialogue with modern culture. Similarly, modernity constitutes the cultural logic of an urban-based industrial capitalism in which highly differentiated structures – political, economic, cultural – increasingly separate themselves from centralised institutions, a process exemplified in Gramsci's concept of civil society and the Frankfurt School's notion of the public sphere. As Kumar notes, modernity is not merely about ideas but embraces intellectual, political and social forms linked historically with capitalist modernisation, industrial technology and economic life – 'a speeding up of economic evolution to the point where it took on revolutionary proportions' (Kumar, 1995, p. 82). But as a process of cultural differentiation, modernity is historically embedded in the dynamics of capitalism and must not be conflated with its modernising infrastructure.

As noted in Chapter 2, Max Weber was the first sociologist to use the term 'modernity' with any degree of precision, but by the end of the nineteenth century it enjoyed a broad popularity and was used widely in the fields of sociology, philosophy, literary criticism and fiction. The historical genesis of the term has been widely discussed, and a number of writers have traced its origins back to the Middle Ages to the concepts of *modernitus* – modern times – and *modernity* – men of today (the philologist Erich Auerbach noted fourteen different meanings in Latin), to the famous seventeenth-century dispute between the 'Ancients' and the 'Moderns' and, more pertinently, to the Rennaissance discovery of time and the differentiation of history into the Ancient, Medieval and Modern periods. By the end of the eighteenth century the concept of society had become rooted in a sense of historical time, its development conceived in terms of a dynamic unfolding process of distinct evolutionary stages (economic for Adam Smith and Adam Ferguson, philosophical and cultural for Kant and Condorcet). The contemporary meaning of modernity is thus imbricated in Enlightenment reason, the belief in progress, empirical science and positivism. Modernity signifies a culture of innovation, a rational ethos challenging traditions and rituals in the name of critical thought, empirical knowledge and humanism.

Historically the concept of modernity belongs to a similar shift of emphasis which Raymond Williams had noted occurring at the end of the eighteenth century when a whole range of new words emerged as part of a changing cultural paradigm seeking to give expression to new modes of experience and social relations:

> The development of *culture* is, perhaps, the most striking among all the words named. It might be said, indeed, that the questions now concentrated in the meanings of the word *culture* are questions directly raised by the great historical changes in *industry*, *democracy* and *class* in their own way represent, and to which the changes in *art* are a closely related response. (Williams, 1961, p. 16)

Modernity had a similar impact, transforming the meaning of the key nineteenth-century words – culture, art, democracy. Other concepts to emerge included alienation, anomie and hegemony, all reflecting changes in the way culture was perceived and theorised. In many ways, modernity was the most elliptical of all these new concepts; it covered a great range of possible meanings and by the end of the nineteenth century had passed into popular usage. Fiction writers, for example, could assume their readers' familiarity with the idea of modernity. In his novel, *Dracula* (1897), Bram Stoker, describing through the words of the English solicitor Jonathan Harker the sinister form of Count Dracula as he leaves his castle to crawl away into the night, notes: 'It is the nineteenth century up-to-date with a vengeance. And yet, unless my senses deceive me, the old centuries had, and have, powers of their own which mere "modernity" cannot kill' (Keating, 1989, p. 350).

Stoker's gothic imagination rekindles the opposition between the archaic and the modern, while other artists, notably Wagner in his operatic cycle, *The Ring of the Nibelung*, fused the two elements into a dynamic aesthetic whole. Both Adorno and Walter Benjamin noted the role played by the archaic in the idea of modernity, with Benjamin drawing a direct comparison between the 'dreamlike' monumental landscape of Haussmann's reconstructed Paris, with its colourful arcades and vast underground catacombes, and ancient Greece, with its monuments and ruins: architecture embodied 'the latent mythology of modernity' within the large and small labyrinth of the metropolis and the arcade (Frisby, 1985, p. 234). A somewhat different rendering was given by Nietzsche, whose writings are infused with the problematic of modernity. In his polemic with Wagner, for example, written after his break with the composer, Nietzsche describes him as 'a decaying and despairing degenerate' whose 'modernity' consists of weaving a seductive concoction of the 'brutal', the 'artificial' and the 'idiotic'. Wagner's music excites 'weary nerves'; he is the 'master of hypnotic tricks'. Wagner's aesthetic 'modernity' constitutes the expression of a 'declining culture', one dominated by the rise of the uneducated, uncultured masses for whom the 'authentic' is both 'superfluous and a liability'. For Nietzsche, Wagner's work gives voice to that 'revolt of the masses' against 'good taste' (Nietzsche, 1967, pp. 179, 183). Through Wagner's music and theatre, modernity finds its most intimate form, 'concealing neither its good nor evil' (ibid., p. 156).

In his work, Nietzsche combines two distinct meanings of modernity. First, modernity as the experience of modern mass democracy in which all living historical forces are drained from culture; and second, modernity as the end of Enlightenment utopianism, the belief in an inevitable progress and scientific reason, modernity as historical pessimism and relativism in which reason becomes 'myth' and culture degenerates into a new bondage of unfreedom. Modernity as democratic levelling and as an iron cage of depersonalised administration are clearly themes which dominate Weberian and Frankfurt School cultural theory.

Before examining these different concepts and theories of modernity, I want to propose three distinct, although overlapping, meanings of modernity and pose the problem of its relevance to a sociology of culture:

1. *Modernity as a literary–aesthetic concept structured in referential discourse with its object as the 'new', the fluid, everchanging and dynamic nature of modern society.* Modernity in this sense negates the concept of the whole, with analysis focusing on the fragmentary and fleeting nature of reality, on the microcosm and the micrological.

2. *Modernity as a sociological–historical category closely linked with the Englightenment 'project' of science and human progress, in which the growing autonomy of knowledge and culture forms the basis of change.* Theorised initially by Weber, this concept of modernity implies a dark side in that the growth of autonomy (in fields or spheres) necessarily leads to a culture of specialists and specialised knowledge, which, as products of Englightenment reason and science, threaten the principle of autonomy and may end with the triumph of formal rationality.

3. *Modernity as a structural concept dealing with the transformation of whole societies, ideologies, social structures and culture.* Modernity confirms the promise of scientific reason to unmask irrational forces and point the way to necessary social change. Modernity thus implies historical awareness, a consciousness of historical continuity and the ways the past continues to live in the present. This concept of modernity emphasises that it is agents and their actions which make history and social change, a process made possible through the specific subjective properties of modernity – increased purposiveness, conscious collective action and the ability to engage in 'reflexive monitoring' in relation to possible alternatives. (Giddens, 1987, p. 223)

This chapter examines these different concepts of modernity in relation to the discussions of culture explored in previous chapters. From Marx to Gramsci, Weber, Simmel and the Frankfurt School the problem of modernity pervades the issues of cultural theory. Moreover, one of the major debates in contemporary social and cultural theory concerns the relation of modernity with post-modernity, raising the question of how far does postmodernity represent a decisive new stage in the development of modern culture.

Modernity 1: From Baudelaire to Foucault

It was the French poet and critic Charles Baudelaire who first used the term modernity with any degree of precision. 'Modernity', he wrote in 1863, 'is the transient, the fleeting, the contingent; it is one half of art, the other being the eternal and immutable.' Writing on contemporary French painting, Baudelaire contrasted the established art of the present, based in old models of classical form, with the 'new' art which engaged directly with modern experience and radical forms, art which distils the poetic and 'epic qualities' of everyday life. The everyday reality of modern experience should exemplify its own 'heroic' features without recourse to classical norms. While contemporary art seeks the ideals of eternal beauty, it does so from within the relativity of the present. Baudelaire describes modernity as the alientated experience of the 'fragmented' nature of modern urban life, what he calls 'the newness of the present' with its 'fleeting moments' suggestive of the eternal captured in the work of certain modern painters and poets.

Modernity is rooted in modern city life, and Baudelaire links his discussion with a number of other concepts such as phantasmagoria, the fleeting moment, 'snapshots' and 'correspondences', all expressing the relations of new forms of fashion, art and architecture to new experiences, feelings and thoughts. He focusses on the figure of the *flaneur*, the dandy, as the embodiment of this new culture, 'haughty', 'patrician' and aggressive, the outsider during a period of historical transformation 'when democracy has not yet become all-powerful, and when aristocracy is only partially weakened and discredited'. The dandy's domain is the crowd:

> His passion and his profession is to merge with the crowd. For the perfect idler, for the passionate observer, it becomes an immense source of enjoyment to establish his dwelling in the throng, in the ebb and flow, the bustle, the fleeting and the infinite.

And his role? To seek 'that indefinable something' called modernity and 'to extract from fashion the poetry which resides in its historical envelope, to distil the eternal from the transitory' (Baudelaire, 1972, pp. 399–421). Thus while the painter of modern life has broken from the past, rejecting tradition in favour of the fragmentary and ephemeral, he or she necessarily seeks the hidden truth which lies below the chaotic and impressionist surface of the everyday.

Baudelaire's modernity is both a subjective response to the emergence of capital cities during a period of rapid industrialisation, with their 'eternal beauty' and remarkable 'harmony' of life, their crowds and movement constituting 'a phantasmagoria of contemporary life', and an objective assessment of the increasing commercialism of culture itself. Modernity signalled a split between culture as the expression of ideal values, and an urban-based mass culture tied to the capitalist market and denigration of autonomous art. Baudelaire was one of the first writers to grasp that the autonomisation of art, which ultimately leads to modernism, was constantly threatened by modern bourgeois society and its culture of mass-produced commodities, hence his support for the avant-garde and quest for the 'new'. But Baudelaire's modernity is static and ahistorical, a concept emptied of historical time. Modernity constitutes a rupture from and not a continuity with the past: all periods thus have their own modernity, as all epochs seek to represent the new.

Excursus: Modernity as Newness in the Present – Foucault on Baudelaire

Baudelaire's modernity forges a new aesthetic from the peculiar features of modern urban life, the concept corresponding to new modes of experience and feeling. Modernity here has no *telos*, it presents no ideals which humanity is seeking to realise, no goals and no purposes. In this sense Baudelaire's modernity is anti-Enlightenment, the opposite of the *philosophes'* belief in inevitable historical progress and autonomy of reason. Thus Foucault takes up Baudelaire's modernity as a critical weapon to be used against the legacy of Enlightenment thought (especially Habermas, the Frankfurt School and all historicist and totalising Marxism).

It should be noted that Foucault is sceptical about the very notion of modernity, and he offers no social theory in which the concept plays any significant role. His account takes the form of a meditation on the significance of Kant's essay, 'What is Enlightenment?' (1784), the starting point for Habermas's analysis of modernity. Foucault follows Baudelaire in defining modernity as primarily

a mode of relating to contemporary reality; a voluntary choice made by certain people; in the end, a way of thinking and feeling; a way, too, of acting and behaving, that at one and the same time marks a relation of belonging and presents itself as a task. (Foucault, 1986, p. 39)

Rather than regarding modernity as an epochal concept, or as a sequel to Enlightenment, Foucault argues that it should be theorised in Kant's terms, referring to a 'present' emptied of future goals and possible transition to a new society. Modernity is rather a way of comprehending the present without recourse to transcendent principles enshrined in concepts such as totality. Rethinking Baudelaire's concept, Foucault defines modernity as the 'will to heroise' the existing present, to grasp its 'high value' and imagine it other than it is. Modernity is not static, but continually defining and renewing itself, not as part of a flux or passing moments, but through the ways individuals relate to the 'newness of the present', the moment of existing – like Baudelaire's dandy, whose ascetism, expressed through his feelings and passions, is modern man striving to 'invent himself', to produce a new and distinctive self. This is Benjamin's understanding of Baudelaire's modernity, the fusion of the archaic and the modern invested with contemporary energy (noted above, pp. 90–1) at work within the epoch which modernity designates (Benjamin, 1983, p. 81). For Foucault, Baudelaire's modernity abhors any finished notion of self, an essence or hidden truth, seeing the active, energising, making side at variance with the notion of modernity as epoch (ibid., p. 41).

Foucault thus accepts what he takes as Baudelaire's way of posing the problem of modernity – what is the meaning of this present? The Enlightenment inaugurated European modernity as rationality, science and the power of knowledge. But in our time, argues Foucault, it is legitimate to ask what remains and what is the meaning of this event. Baudelaire has posed the problem of modernity against the grain of totalising theories: and Weber's emphasis on cultural meanings produced within specific contexts by agents (contradicting his metanarrative of the iron cage of rationality) is closely linked with Baudelaire's project. Self, energy, microcosm: this is Foucault's rendering of modernity. Yet Foucault fails to contextualise these ideas, for self and energy do not materialise out of the air of modernity but are structured in institutions, social relations and specific positions within particular fields. Foucault's analysis highlights the strengths and weaknesses of Baudelaire's modernity, its repudiation of a finalising discourse of cultural development, its sense of culture as contained within a timeless present.

David Frisby has noted how Baudelaire's concept of modernity proved an important source for the development of a social theory of modernity, especially in the work of Simmel and the Frankfurt School (notably Benjamin and Kracauer, who adopted a micrological rather than a totalising approach). A social theory of modernity came to concentrate on the social and cultural upheavals caused by rapid capitalist economic development and corresponding new modes of perception and experience of time and space as transitory, fleeting, fortuitous or arbitrary. Simmel shares many of Baudelaire's concepts (on fragmentation, experience and micrological analysis) and represents a bridge between the literary–aesthetic notion of modernity and a sociologically grounded concept.

Simmel's Modernity

Simmel shares Baudelaire's anti-holism. Describing society as a labyrinth or web of interactions, Simmel analysed 'sociation' as a process involving individuals as both products and the makers of society. For Simmel, the real life of any modern society was concentrated in 'microscopic molecular processes', or microscopic interaction such as social gatherings and small social groups, and not in large-scale social formations. Simmel defines modernity in terms of patterns of social interaction and sociation which correspond directly with Simmel's analyses of fashion, for example, in terms both of its transitory and its eternal qualities, fashion seeking to signify the universal while simultaneously embracing the practical and the utilitarian.

But the heart of Simmel's analysis of modernity lies in his exhaustive study of the role played by money in modern society. Money generates social differentiation, reduces everything to fragments. Modernity is theorised as a social world dominated by the exchange and circulation of commodities, a culture characterised by monetary ties and relationships. Money has the effect of reducing the qualitative nature of objects to one of mere economic exchange:

> This is certainly a deep reason for the problematic character, the restlessness and the dissatisfaction of our times. The qualitative nature of objects lose their psychological emphasis through the money economy;

the continuously required estimation according to monetary value eventually causes this to seem the only valid one; more and more, people speed
past the specific value of things, which cannot be expressed in terms of
money. (Simmel, 1991, p. 23)

The 'core of meaning' slips through one's fingers as 'the innermost
value of things suffers under the uniform convertability of the most
heterogeneous elements into money'. The abstract dominance of
money becomes the foundation of the culture of modernity. Human
relations increasingly revolve around the dominant motifs of the
culture – punctuality, exactness, pecuniary considerations – a social
world built on the reification of objects, indifferent and colourless,
generating quantitative not qualitative values. Culture can no longer
function to unify society for, lacking universal values and meaning it
becomes impersonal, external, dominated by innumerable commodities that lead to a phantasmagoric and closed reality.

In his essay on 'The Berlin Trade Fair' (1896), Simmel describes the
effect that a commodity-dominated culture exerts on 'overstimulated
and tired nerves' as individuals reach out for any form of excitement:

it appears as though modern man's one-sided and monotonous role in the
division of labour will be compensated for by consumption and enjoyment
through the growing pressure of heterogeneous impressions, and the ever
faster and more colourful change of excitements. The differentiation of the
active side of life is apparently complemented through the extensive diversity of its passive and receiving side. (Simmel, 1991, p. 120)

Simmel analyses the growth of large-scale trade exhibitions as
emblematic of modern culture as they momentarily constitute the
'centre of world civilisation' to form a 'totality of cultural production'.
While such a totality is suggestive of 'outward unity', the 'flux of forces
at work' generates contradictions, notably in the plurality of styles and
objects. Nothing can claim permanence and durability.

At the centre of Simmel's theory of modernity lies an unresolved
tension between opposing elements, the universal and the transitory,
the active and passive elements of human action. For while his sociology is built around the processes of interaction and a non-reified
notion of the social, it remains an interaction without a cultural agent.
Modernity is not made: it is the tragic acceptance of a world of
fragments and ephemeral experiences.

In the essay on urbanism, for example, Simmel argues that the growth of the modern city encourages the development of individuality, autonomy and personal freedom through expanding the forms of social interaction, but simultaneously it generates impersonality and social isolation. Similarly, the division of labour, while encouraging narrow specialisms which enhance individuality, has the effect of promoting anonymity, engulfing the individual in a world of objects and reducing him to a mere cog in 'the vast, overwhelming organisation of things... and forces which gradually take out of his hands everything connected with progress, spirituality and value' (Simmel, 1950).

Although Simmel has been widely praised in recent years for his writings on modernity, his analysis remains deeply problematic. As I have argued, Simmel's cultural sociology is vitiated by the rigid dichotomy he develops between culture as the expression of interiority and authority, and culture as external, impersonal and reified forms. Thus while sharing Baudelaire's emphasis on the fragment and the micrological, Simmel's modernity departs radically from Baudelaire through grounding modernity in the metanarrative of an irreconcilable tragedy of culture, its failure to generate unity in the face of commodity fetishism and reification. The individual is fated to tragic resignation and passivity. Simmel's modernity lacks reflexivity: there is no sense in individuals interacting dialogically, as active producers of culture. To use Bourdieu's expression, Simmel's modernity is dominated by the short circuit effect: culture defined without links to the micro elements, institutions and agents, culture emptied of all communicative relations and historical forces.

Modernity 2: Critique of Enlightenment – From Weber to the Frankfurt School

The Baudelaire–Simmel theorisation of modernity, based on the category of experience and micrological analysis, falters over the question posed by Foucault, the relation of agent to the different forms of modernity and the possibility of action. Simmel's modernity encloses an irreconcilable dualism between the fixed nature of the agent (Simmel has no conception of habitus, for example) and the inflexible, externalised nature of culture. Simmel advances no theory of communication, the active specifics of social interaction, such as language, which form a bridge between objective culture (Bourdieu's field) and subjective culture (internalised by the agent); his concept of modernity lacks any historical momentum, little sense of historical time and any structural analysis other than a generalised emphasis on the experience of the money economy, urbanism and the circulation of commodities. In sharp contrast, Weber advanced a concept of modernity both structural and normative enmeshed with a critique of Enlightenment philosophy which goes beyond Simmel's fixed antinomies. Weber's sociology theorises a more complex account of the structural forces at work within modern culture which generate the possibility of autonomy, freedom and differentiation.

The normative meaning of Weber's modernity derives in part from Nietzsche's reflections on modern history and culture. For Nietzsche, modernity pointed to the emergence of a 'sick society' in which 'true cultural achievement' becomes increasingly undermined by growing commercialism and mass democracy. The legacy of the Enlightenment lay in the triumph of scientistic thought and the abolition of any real sense of the 'eternal'. Enlightenment science leads to the domination of positivism with its basis in the facticity of the social world in which surface constitutes the living reality. Moreover, positivism advocated the idea of system and holistic thought: 'I mistrust all systematisers and avoid them. The will to a system is a lack of integrity' (Nietzsche, 1990, p. 35). Although Weber shared Nietzsche's hostility to holistic concepts, he nevertheless pursued the idea of historical narrative, a metanarrative of history in which the ideal of rationality becomes an iron cage of depersonalised administration and authority. For Nietzsche, the emphasis lay on the 'moment' and the 'fragment' as the only modes of affirming the possibility of the eternal. Fragments and moments are irreducible, providing meaning in a world progressively emptied of meaning. Holistic thought is clearly the enemy: the concept of totality is false. Hence Nietzsche's rejection of linear history and the progressive unfolding of immanent values: history is exhausted, and there are no universal values, only a culture saturated with a medley of opposing values and ideologies. Modernity has no inner core of meaning, it possesses neither goal nor purpose, embodying only the inevitable recurrence of sameness (or 'nothingness'). Enlightenment philosophy had effectively emptied history of will, energy and power.

Weber's concept of modernity develops out of these Nietzschean themes – the pluralism of values, an open rather than a teleological concept of historical development, a profound pessimism over the potential for autonomy and freedom in a modern industrialised society, individualising rather than totalising concepts – as he depicts the progessive rationalisation of the social world through the motivation and action of particular agents (the Protestant ethic thesis, see Chapter 2). Through the energy and will of purposive rational action, the process of rationality spreads from its origins in the religious sphere to other spheres, including the political (the state, bureaucracy), culture, law and human personality. Thus the economic sphere becomes autonomous through this rationalisation process, separated from the political sphere, and distinguished by its own internal logic, that is, business conducted on the basis of impersonal rules, on calculation and discipline; the principles of coherence and consistency replace the irrational and personal elements of pre-modernity in which the economic and political were combined.

The structural basis of modernity stems from the disintegration of the pre-modern homogeneous world of unified ideologies and the development of a plurality of rationalised, differentiated and competing autonomous spheres. This is a modernity dominated by the rational choice of ends, calculation of the most efficient means to achieve specific ends, and rational action guided by knowledge and values. In his 'Intermediate Reflections' (1915), Weber makes clear that there should be no mixing of values internal to a particular sphere, so that the values specific to the political sphere, for example, should in no way enter and legitimate the artistic and aesthetic sphere; the cultural must be clearly distinguished from the political and economic. Weber's modernity is thus opposed to that process of the 'aestheticisation of politics' which took place under the Nazis, in staged festivals and mass cultural rallies, and the fusion of art and politics characteristic of modern totalitarian cultures. The separation of spheres constitutes the promise of Enlightenment, notably Kant's three spheres of science, morality (including law) and art, and Weber links the principle of autonomy with socio-historical change – the decentring of world views – which enables individuals to produce meanings free of centralised authority (Weber, 1948, p. 328).

Modernity is thus the relation of humanity to the rationalised and autonomous spheres which provides the possibility of rational action. But the autonomy of spheres is threatened by the forces of rationality itself. As noted in Chapter 2, Weber's concept of rationality combines both emancipatory (substantive) and utilitarian elements (formal). The tension between the substantive rationality of 'ultimate ends', namely justice, equality and freedom, values which give life its meaning, and the formal rationality of law, bureaucracy and specialised knowledge, disciplines necessary for the efficient functioning of a modern society (built around the values of calculation and impersonality), becomes the signature of modernity. Each sphere requires both specialised knowledge and specialists whose role is to legislate on specific issues. Without such specialists there can be no autonomy; but such autonomy may be based in formal not substantive rationality. Formal rationality perfects the major institutions and practices of capitalism, the free market and its administrative apparatus, and threatens the emancipatory potential inherent in the spheres themselves. Formal rationality fits individuals to a system of predetermined ends, transforming them into anonymous units of depersonalised domination.

The dialectic of modernity, then, leads ultimately to the 'disenchantment of the world' and the eclipse of hope for a rationally organised and free society. The differentiation of spheres suggests autonomy and freedom, but the inherent conflict between formal and substantive rationality leads Weber to deeply pessimistic conclusions. However, Weber's differentiation thesis marks an advance in the analysis of modernity, and it is this the Frankfurt School take up in their work.

Theorising Modernity: The Frankfurt School

In the *Dialectic of Enlightenment* (1944), Adorno and Horkheimer, writing under the shadow of totalitarianism as the dominant tendency of modern culture, took up Weber's paradox that the process of rationalisation connoted both freedom–emancipation and bondage–reification. The *Dialectic of Enlightenment* focusnes on the genesis of bourgeois culture, but goes beyond Weber by tracing its origins to ancient Greece and the account of myth in Homer's *Odyssey*. The goals of Enlightenment philosophy and science lay in secularising, 'disenchanting and demythologising the social world' through the dissolution of myths, replacing 'fortuitious insights' with scientific knowledge. But Adorno and Horkheimer set out to show how myth and Enlightenment are closely entangled, so that the mythological world of the Odyssey implies enlightenment.

The *Odyssey* constitutes a basic text of European civilisation, show-
ing the ways in which the subject emancipates itself from the domination of myth by cunning and reason. Homer's poem, while rooted in a
mythological age, seeks the destruction of myth with Odysseus,
depicted by Adorno and Horkheimer as a Robinson Crusoe figure,
forced by circumstances to pursue 'atomistic' interests which embody
'the principle of capitalist economy', that is, risk-taking in pursuit of
success (Adorno and Horkheimer, 1973, pp. 61–2). From the *Odyssey*
onwards, Enlightenment constitutes attempts by individuals to free
themselves from the domination of nature through rational principles.
But Adorno and Horkheimer go further than Weber in seeing
Enlightenment as a modernity split in two. For them, Enlightenment
is as 'totalitarian as any system', through its organising elements of
calculation, quantification, formalism, utility and efficiency. The
Enlightenment principles of order, control, domination and system
banish all myth, subjectivity and value, with its ideal 'the system from
which all and everything follows'. Formal rationality thus provides
Enlightenment with the 'schema of the calculability of the world'
(ibid., pp. 3–7). The totalitarian implications of Enlightenment find
their most complete expression in the concept of culture industry,
which transforms the liberating, civilising potential of communication
into a conformist and passive mode of total administration and control.

In his critique of the *Dialectic of Enlightenment*, Habermas has
argued that Adorno and Horkheimer oversimplified the image of
modernity and failed to do justice to 'the rational content of cultural
modernity' exemplified in bourgeois ideals. Adorno and Horkheimer
ignored the fundamental elements of cultural modernity, which suggest alternatives to the pervasive domination of purposive formal
rationality. The *Dialectic of Enlightenment* remains rooted in a deterministic, tragic and pessimistic perspective. The development of
autonomous spheres and experts does not necessarily suggest the
triumph of instrumental rationality, for the 'validity claims' made by
and mediated by specialists must justify the specific principles and
practices inherent in each sphere. The values of each sphere are not
automatically legitimated: they must be argued over in critical discourse and command consensus from non-specialists. In short, Habermas argues that the real potential of each sphere lies in going beyond
mere technical and formal knowledge to raise issues which strike at

the foundations of modern culture, problems of law and morality, political constitutions, economic organisation and aesthetic forms. The result is the production of substantive, not formal, values as, for example, in the discourses of specialised art or aesthetic criticism which may raise problems of the cultural value of particular art practices. It is this unfulfilled emancipatory core of Enlightenment which Adorno and Horkheimer ignored.

In arguing for the 'project of modernity', Habermas follows Weber in identifying three autonomous spheres – science, morality and art – each with a specific internal rationality. Weber's concept of modernity emphasised the growing authority of specialised knowledge inherent in this differentiation process and a developing gap between 'experts' and the public. But Weber's pessimism obscured the inherent emancipatory potential of Enlightenment:

> The project of modernity formulated in the eighteenth century by the philosophers of the Enlightenment consisted of their efforts to develop objective science, universal morality and law, and autonomous art according to their inner logic. At the same time, this project intended to release the cognitive potentials of each of these domains from their esoteric forms. The Enlightenment philosophers wanted to utilise this accumulation of specialised culture for the enrichment of everyday life – that is to say, for the rational organisation of everyday social life. (Habermas, 1985, p. 9)

Thus the accumulated knowledge of the three spheres does not automatically lead to the enslavement of humanity; rather it opens up the inherent possibilities of the social and cultural world. But this is only feasible if Weber's model and that of Adorno and Horkheimer incorporate a theory of communicative action based on collective practices which enables the project to be realised through relinking modern culture with everyday life. Both the critique of Weber and that of Adorno and Horkheimer blunt the emancipatory logic of rationality by a 'totalising repudiation of modern forms of life' (such as bureaucratic and total administration), thus reducing the prospects of 'self-conscious practice', self-development' and 'self-realisation'. Hence the sphere of art can generate the radical power of avant-garde art with its subversive critique of tradition, while the specialised activity of art criticism produces values critical of the existing social order.

For Habermas, the rationalisation and differentiation of spheres, with their concomitant specialised culture, opens the way to the production of knowledge, criticism and communication. Moreover, this normative content of modernity effectively becomes part of the life-world, entering institutions and helping to shape different cultural practices. The emancipatory potential of modernity is nowhere better exemplified than in the work of Bakhtin with its critique of finalising monologic discourses and its celebration of dialogic and decentred discourses and the hybrid, heteroglossic nature of culture. In contrast, the Frankfurt School's notion of culture industry narrows and impoverishes the content of modernity, imprisoning the individual within a closed administered world impervious to change. Specialised knowledge must always remain sensitive to the 'highly ambivalent' content of cultural modernity (Habermas, 1987, p. 338).

The value of Habermas's defence of Weber's thesis lies in its clear grasp of the historical and cultural specifics of modernity, grounding it in a theory of historical change. But it is precisely this argument on the progressive rationalisation of Western society which has promoted suspicion and criticism, which point to the totalising principles inherent in Habermas's notion. Postmodern theorists reject the Enlightenment concept of modernity, with its emphasis on the burgeoning authority of knowledge, science and technology, because of its levelling and homogenising of culture, which drown and marginalise other voices and standpoints. Differences are eliminated. Foucault further dismissed the idea of 'a unique form of rationality' in favour of different rationalities at work within multiple, interconnected fields. Moreover, there exists no general law which links together these different forms of rationality.

While Habermas defends the project of Englightenment, Foucault abandons it. He rejects every global, totalising mode of thought in which society is conceived as a whole, the constituent parts unified by the presence of a dominant centre, an essence, a *telos*. Society is, rather, theorised micrologically in terms of a fragmented field of disconnected discourses. Systematising theories grounded in concepts such as continuity, genesis, totality and the subject cannot uncover the workings of multiple discourses within a field of knowledge. Both Baudelaire and Nietzsche are thus exemplars of modernity because of their emphasis on the microcosm and the fragmentary. Baudelaire's exaltation of the present at the expense of historical memory, of many modernities rather than one, leads to the rejection of tradition and any sense of historical continuity. Nietzsche's work further advances the principles of discontinuity and dispersion rather than continuity and identity, heterogeneity and pluralism rather than homogeneity.

The problem with Foucault's analysis lies in its failure to contextualise the decentring and micrological processes, to provide the infrastructure of the 'fragment' and the 'dispersal' of elements. As I have argued, Weber advances a concept of modernity as a structured process in which the principle of autonomy is historically contextualised, albeit abstractly. But Foucault succeeds only in reducing culture to discourse, severing the many living, historical links between the different discourses, the collective agents who make and remake them, and the complex patterns of communication which render them as practices. Thus while Foucault remains hostile to metanarratives and subject-centred explanations, his work constitutes an intellectual cul-de-sac, one incapable of generating analytical concepts which situate or contextualise modernity (without finality, open and decentred in the Bakhtinian mode, for example) as a process involving reflexive agents. Moreover, the differentiation of cultural fields implies hierarchy, power and influence, the possibility that some cultural practices and specialised knowledge are more significant and dominant than others. It is this aspect of modernity, its sociological core, that eludes Foucault and, as was suggested in Chapter 4, suggests limitations to Habermas's model of communicative rationality and his theory of modernity.

Modernity 3: Marx

As one of the key elements in the theory of modern culture, the concept of modernity belongs more to the sociological tradition of Weber and Simmel than to Marxism. In general, those Marxist theorists who developed a concept of modernity, such as Adorno and Benjamin, remained sceptical of Marx's materialism (especially the role allocated to collective social labour in social development) and his related methodology based in the category of totality. Habermas follows Adorno in rejecting Marx's concept of labour in favour of a theory of communication and language; and while Benjamin's highly influential work has been widely discussed, its focus on the micrological and the philosophically interpretative seem to have only the most tenuous links with Marx.

Yet Benjamin and Adorno, as well as Weber and Simmel, all claim some kinship of ideas with Marx. In what sense is there a theory of modernity in Marx's writings? In recent years a number of writers have attempted to distil such a theory from Marx, notably Marshall Berman's *All That is Solid Melts into Air* (1983), which identifies a bridge between Marx and Baudelaire in that both emphasise the dynamic principles inherent in the present, its disruptions and discontinuities, its revolutionary character and subversion of tradition.

Berman's view of modernity is based on the idea of human action and social change. To comprehend fully what is meant by modernity means abandoning all theories which reduce the agent to a passive status. He argues that much of contemporary cultural theory, especially structuralism and postmodernism, has got rid of the active agent, the relation of self to the existing society and, more pertinently, to history. He cites Foucault as an exemplary instance for, although writing extensively on the problem of modernity, Foucault insists that human beings have no role to play in the construction of the social and cultural world, his work resonating 'an endless, excruciating series of variations on the Weberian themes of the iron cage and human nullities whose souls are shaped to fit the bars' (Berman, 1983, pp. 33–4). Berman further argues that contemporary social theory has abandoned a sense of wholeness, so that modernity bifurcates into two distinct concepts, modernism and modernisation, the aesthetic–artistic and the societal. It is a split which Marx's work rejects.

Drawing almost entirely on *The Communist Manifesto*, Berman describes the expansion of capitalist production as a global phenomenon with the emergence of a world market and highly centralised fiscal and administrative structures, all of which tend to undermine both the effectiveness of the nation state as well as local industries and markets. But in revolutionising capitalist production, the bourgeoisie go further, transforming culture itself and with it human wants, capacities and desires. What matters to Marx, Berman writes, 'is the processes, the powers, the expressions of human life and energy: men working, moving, cultivating, communicating, organising and reorganising nature and themselves...' (ibid., p. 93). The revolutionary economic dynamic of modern capitalism penetrates deeply into personal and social life, transforming institutions, practices and traditions. In Marx's (and Engels's words):

Constant revolutionising of production, uninterrupted disturbance of all
social relations, everlasting uncertainty and agitation, distinguish the bourgeois epoch from all earlier times. All fixed, fast-frozen relationships...are
swept away, all newly formed ones become obsolete before they can ossify.
All that is solid melts into air, all that is holy is profaned, and men at last
are forced to face with sober senses the real conditions of their lives and
their relations with their fellow men. (Marx and Engels, 1958, p. 37)

Berman's main point is that capitalism creates the possibility for the
genuine enlargement of humanity while simultaneously destroying its
basis in a division of labour which fosters alienation, fragmentation
and partially developed human beings. At the same time, modern
developments within industry demand high levels of skill and cooperation, so that individuals are increasingly taught to act and think
collectively. Modern bourgeois civilisation is thus a culture characterised by insecurity and revolutionary activity, one in which the
burgeoning working-class movement must eventually generate communism, although Berman notes that this might 'stifle the active,
dynamic and developmental forces that have brought it into being'
thus betraying the hopes and possibilities for an egalitarian and con-
flict-free society.

   For Berman, Marx's is a 'melting vision', in which the apparent
solidity of bourgeois society is progressively undermined by shocks
and collisions, 'permanent upheavals in every sphere of life, crises and
contradictions, demonic and terrifying, swinging wildly out of control,
menacing and destroying blindly as it moves'. Berman depicts Marx as
a modernist using language and images that portray

   the glory of modern energy and dynamism, the ravages of modern disintegration and nihilism...a vortext where all facts and values are whirled,
   exploded and decomposed, recombined; a basic uncertainty about what is
   basic, what is valuable, even what is real. (ibid., p. 121)

Berman, then, links Marx with an aesthetic discourse on modernity.
But this emphasis on Marx's modernism is at odds with Marx's work
as a whole, especially his studies of the historical nature of modern
capitalism and its 'laws of motion', his analysis of the structural
dynamics lying below the surface of specific events, to link capitalist
'energy' and dynamism with more permanent and determining forces.
The key to Marx's notion of modernity lies not so much in the

polemical stance of *The Communist Manifesto*, but rather in the rich and complex analyses of capitalism as a social system. The *Communist Manifesto* represents Marx in polemical mood: it is a text which urges collective action, a rallying point for the oppressed and a blueprint for revolutionary practice. As a text it necessarily advanced a simplified analysis of capitalism (a society consisting of two antagonistic social classes, for example). But many of Marx's fundamental concepts essential for the analysis of capitalism as a system are missing or undertheorised. It was only in his later work – notably the *Grundrisse* and *Capital* – that Marx's emphasis shifts to defining labour as labour-power, a unique commodity found only within the capitalist mode of production. In *The Communist Manifesto* labour is characterised as 'abstract, general and social labour', an approach which succeeded in mystifying the precise relation between the creation of value (expressed in money, for example) and human activity (expressed in labour). Labour-power constitutes a commodity; labour in general does not. The creation of wealth is possible only through the exploitation of labour-power, the transformation of labour from an affirmation to a denial of human values. Thus in *Capital* Marx argues that commodity production entails the separation of two specific kinds of value, exchange and use value, values which either command a price or satisfy a human and social need. The commodity combines both use and exchange value, a 'basic' contradiction which embodies the conditions necessary for capitalist development. The worker exists only to satisfy the demands of the economic system; material wealth does not exist to satisfy the needs of the worker's development. The social process of production effectively negates the need for community, and cooperation and human relationships become 'atomised', assuming a material character independent of human control and conscious activity (Marx, 1958, ch. xxxvi). 'The total movement of this disorder is its order' (Marx and Engels, 1958, p. 77).

The social bond which links the individual to society is thus expressed in exchange value, so much so that 'the individual carries his social power, as well as his bond with society, in his pocket' (Marx, 1973, pp. 156–7). Money becomes the objective bond of society, the real community in a system dominated by exchange values. The result is a mystification of the unequal relation of capital to labour, and in a famous passage Marx writes of the commodity as 'a mysterious thing' which disguises the social character of labour, presenting the relations between the producers and the totality of their labour 'as a social relation, existing not between themselves, but between the products of their labour'. Social relations are inverted, so that 'every element, even the simplest, the commodity for example...causes relations between people to appear as attributes of things'. The social world of modern capitalism is thus a perverted world in which the products of labour generate an apparent independence, so that objects 'rule the producers instead of being ruled by them', while those engaged in production 'live in a bewitched world', in which their own relationships appear 'as properties of things...of the material elements of production'. Humanity becomes increasingly dominated by a world of things, by processes its own activity has created but which, through the workings of the capitalist economic system, turn against it, as objective, external forces (Marx, 1958, pp. 72–3). Social wealth becomes an 'alien and dominant power...a monstrous objective power which, created through social labour, belongs not to the worker but...to capital'. The emphasis, Marx notes, is 'not on the state of being *objectified*, but...of being *alienated*, dispossessed, sold' (Marx, 1973, pp. 831–2). A mystical veil obscures the real foundations.

Marx's language, here, is in sharp contrast to that of *The Communist Manifesto*: in *Capital* and in the *Grundrisse* he is concerned with capitalism as a specific historical social formation, systematically structured through crises, tensions and contradictions. It is the latter which constitute the key to Marx's notion of modernity: for while capitalism fragments, alienates and atomises individuals, erodes community and social bonds, such social forms are linked with the underlying logic of capitalism as an economic system. Unlike Berman, Marx does not reduce modernity to a mental climate or the experiences of atomised and alienated agents. Terms such as fleeting and fragmentary, discontinuity and disintegration must be linked with specific economic and social conditions, a context in which individuals experience culture in this way. Berman advances subjective categories with little analytical value. In contrast, Marx sees modernity in terms of an objective historical process grounded in the laws of commodity production and the overwhelming power of money over human life.

An example of the integral relation between system and experience is Marx's analysis of the notion of fragmentation. Individuals experience the sense of alienation and fragmentation through the position they occupy within the highly organised and disciplined capitalist division of labour, which effectively separates the mass of direct producers from control over the means of production. Similarly, system imperatives such as the credit system, which coordinate and regulate capital flows to specific branches of industry, assume the practices of financial speculation and thus economic–social crises: coordinating systems should function to regulate and bring order to the investment of capital, but as David Harvey points out, there is at work a central contradiction in that 'credit creation and disbursement can never be separated from speculation'. A permanent tension characterises the relation of the financial system to its monetary basis. At no point is there a guarantee that the system works to satisfy human needs and wants, with capital finding its way, for example, into new housing and industries. Capital restlessly searches for new profitable markets irrespective of human need, its investments geared to surplus value. The social consequences may result in fragmentation and loss of community and a problematical social order.

Marx's concept of modernity, then, is system-based, linked with the objective laws of capitalist development and contradictions between the forces and relations of production. The reappearance of the archaic, the past, makes sense in these terms. For the logic of capitalist economics leads to the possibility of social disintegration and thus the necessity for legitimating ideas and alternative notions of community. Capitalist modernity constantly throws up the spirits and myths of the past, cultural traditions which seek to establish viable social bonds. Phantasmagoric forms veil the structural contradictions and crises: to situate modernity on the surface through 'experience' divests it of its historical roots in exploitation and the underlying logic of system forces. But such analysis poses two problems: first, the principle of the autonomy of culture is left untheorised and, second, the role played by the agent or self remains problematic. In other words, while Marx's approach provides the basis for a structural explanation of the experience of modernity, it does not address the problem of the cultural logic of modernity itself. As was argued in Chapter 1, Marx's work oscillates between functionalist and dialectical explanation. While his account of modernity is structural and historical, there remains the problem of finalising discourses, the role of dominant ideology in culture, for example, the unity of culture as against its hybrid forms, its closed rather than open, dialogic modes. These and other problems are examined in the next chapter on the post-modern critique of modernity.

Chapter 9

Postmodernity and Mass Culture

As I have argued, Marx locates capitalism as a specific economic system contextually and historically, its structure analysed in terms of a hierarchy of elements centred around imperatives of production. Specific laws – those relating to the centralisation of production, the fusion of finance and industrial capital, the falling rate of profit – regulate its internal workings. While the logic of capitalism appears anarchic – individuals pursuing their own selfish interests within a market situation – the inevitable destruction of old communities and traditions, history as a set of random events – there exists an underlying structure based in system logic and historical necessity. Marx advances a coherent historical narrative in which antagonistic social classes struggle for power and legitimacy in order to impose their own ideology on the whole of society. As one of the master narratives of modernity, capitalist industrialisation has as its agents the internal contradictions of the system itself.

Such grand narratives characterise sociological, Marxist and philosophical discourses on modernity: Weber and Durkheim portray history as narratives of rationalisation and the unfreedom of the iron cage, the triumph of organic solidarity over anomie; Gramsci, too, narrates the historical transcendence of narrow class interests and ideology through the hegemonic accession of a universal culture.

Critique of Modernity I: The Postmodern and the Grand Narrative

Belonging firmly to the era of modernity, these grand narratives have been judged redundant. With the dominant Marxist narrative of emancipation in his sights, the postmodern philosopher Lyotard argues that the persistence of struggles against communism from within communist states has rendered such narratives 'barely credible' (Lyotard, 1989, p. 318). Lyotard's hugely influential *The Postmodern Condition* was first published in 1979 (and translated into English in 1984), and although much of the argument owes a debt to French post-structuralism – the death of the subject, the priority given to language and language games in the construction of reality – its basic thrust is against Enlightenment reason, universal history and the concept of totality: 'Let us wage war on totality', he declares, on all attempts to forge order and sense out of the flux of multiple and discontinuous events. Such totalising history and metanarratives include the Marxist thesis of 'emancipation from exploitation and alienation through the socialisation of labour', and Habermas's narrative of emancipation through the ideal speech community and undistorted communication (ibid., p. 315).

Lyotard defines postmodernity precisely as an 'incredulity towards metanarratives' while modernity designates 'any science that legitimates itself with reference to a metadiscourse', such as the Enlightenment's appeal to the goal of universal freedom. Such meta-narratives are rooted in a nostalgic yearning for organic unity, whole-ness, harmony. But there is no collective, universal subject seeking emancipation and freedom. The concept of the whole is totalitarian and 'terroristic' in that it seeks to exclude others from participating in its idealised community. Metanarratives always appeal to the interests of particular communities with their basis in homogeneity and com-mon purpose. Thus Habermas's notion of consensus is dismissed as 'outmoded' and 'suspect' guaranteeing not freedom but the end of independent and critical thought. For Lyotard, the heterogeneity of language games, their diversity, dissensus and constant struggle neces-sarily produce indeterminacy and ambiguity.

There are clear echoes in Lyotard's analysis of modernity of the Frankfurt School's critique of Enlightenment as well as of Bakhtin's notion of finalising monologic discourses which strive to homogenise and close off all alternative and oppositional voices. But Lyotard's philosophical critique of modernity makes no attempt to contextualise and situate ideas historically and provide any analysis of the conditions which generate and sustain cultural diversity and openness. Or, rather, Lyotard argues that pluralism and difference arise out of language and aesthetics, and especially through the avant-garde with its commitment to experiment. The postmodern is thus that 'which denies itself the solace of good forms, the consensus of a taste which would make it possible to share collectively the nostalgia for the unattainable'. The postmodern writer works without pre-established rules and categories, in order to 'formulate the rules of what will have been done'.

Thus, although a critique of social, political and historical theories, Lyotard's work is narrowly conceived as an interpretation of cultural forms and ideas separated from their basis in social and economic structures. Because he has abandoned the representations and truths of the grand narratives, Lyotard rejects all modes of representation, objective meaning and truth. Only by negating the ossified forms of modernity and modernism can the postmodern define itself, for 'a work can become modern only if it is at first postmodern'.

Lyotard has defined modernity in narrow and impoverished terms, stripping it of those elements which enable agents to engage in purposive action within an open, pluralist culture. It is true that some versions of modernity suggest enclosure and assimilation of difference to an underlying uniform culture – culture industry, Parsonian common culture – a standpoint which homogenises the concept of modernity. Culture as the realm of meanings, action, purpose and value lies at the heart of the modernity project: to theorise society and culture as wholes does not imply teleological determinism, for wholes can coexist with difference, diversity and openness, elements made by participants or agents whose actions constitute wholes.

Critique of Modernity 2: Postmodernism and Culture

The concept of modernity arose initially as both Enlightenment optimism and Baudelairian 'newness', the disruption of tradition by the avant-garde and quest for new aesthetic forms. The concept of the postmodern similarly emerges when modernism seems exhausted and no longer capable of dealing with the 'newness' of modern mass society. As the aesthetic wing of modernity, modernism is identified with a privileged discourse in which high culture embodies the realm of authenticity, and popular mass culture the realm of alienation and inauthenticity.

In her book, *The Post-Modern and the Post-Industrial*, Margaret Rose has traced the origins of the postmodern to a variety of intellectual contexts, including history (Arnold Toynbee's *Study of History*, 1939, which identified the postmodern with the rise of the industrial working class and modernism with the middle class), literature (notably Latin American poetry during the 1940s) and sociology (C. Wright Mills's *The Sociological Imagination*, 1959, which refers to a Fourth epoch as the postmodern following the Modern Age). None of these usages, however, theorised the postmodern with any rigour, and only in architecture was the postmodern analysed as a new and distinctive aesthetic closely linked with modern mass culture. In 1945 the architect Joseph Hudnut used the concept to refer to mass-produced, prefabricated housing designed to allow every family 'its standardised and mass-produced shell indistinguishable from those of its thousand neighbours...' As Rose points out, although the post-modern had been used before, Hudnut specifically designated 'an ultra-functionalist version of the modern house', emphasising standardisation and mechanisation as ends in themselves and thus separate from cultural and aesthetic issues. Unlike the modernist architecture of the Bauhaus, with its consciously defined utopian goals of renewing urban space by fostering a sense of community, belonging and whole-ness, post-modernist architecture accepted the fragmentation caused by the capitalist division of labour and society as a hierarchically structured system of class inequality. While the modernist aesthetics of the Bauhaus challenged the crude materialism of capitalism and sought to break down class divisions through socially mixed housing and highly individualised artefacts, post-modern architecture defined its role as providing the new owners with a culture 'free from all sentimentality or fantasy or caprice' with their 'habits of thought...-most necessary to a collective-industrial scheme of life' (Rose, 1991).

As the idea of the postmodern became increasingly used during the 1950s, the term came to signify the eclipse of the modern in favour of the popular. As with the idea of modernity, the postmodern formed part of specific literary–aesthetic discourse, although its origins lay in architecture and history. Literary critics such as Irving Howe, Leslie Fiedler and Harry Levin defined the postmodern as a distinctly new literary form which eroded the fixed boundaries between the popular and modern, between popular culture and modernist sensibility. The novels of J. D. Salinger (*The Catcher in the Rye*), Norman Mailer (*The Deer Park*) and Jack Kerouac (*On the Road*) depict a social world which appears increasingly shapeless and full of ambiguity. The old, stable assumptions of fiction no longer seemed relevant, and in responding to the realities of modern mass society the postmodern writers rejected realist 'portraiture' in favour of fable, prophecy, nostalgia and the picaresque mode. The postmodern anti-hero supplants the problematic hero of modernism, rootless and alienated. Howe makes the point that the early postmodern writers tended to an uncritical, largely passive acceptance of this new, amorphous mass society. Society, wrote Howe, is now one in which 'the population grows passive, indifferent and atomised; in which traditional loyalties, ties and associations become lax or dissolve entirely... in which man becomes a consumer, himself mass-produced like the products, diversions and values that he absorbs' (Howe, 1992).

Conceived in this way, the postmodern forecloses the possibility of a utopian and liberating potential in popular culture. Leslie Fiedler argued that the turn to the postmodern inaugurated a more active, involved public, one which refused instruction and education 'from above', from critics and teachers of high art, turning rather to popular genres (the western, science fiction etc.) in which there were neither 'leaders of taste' nor 'followers'. Popular art, he suggests, regardless of its overt politics, is always subversive, 'a threat to all hierarchies in so far as it is hostile to order and ordering in its own realm'. The postmodern implies 'the closing of the gap between artist and audience', for literature now speaks 'the language of everyone' and not simply that of a 'cultivated élite' and in a secular age 'becomes again prophetic and universal' (Fiedler, 1992). For many other writers the postmodern signified a genuine tendency towards a democratic, open culture that would finally put the lid on elitist, closed modernity. One of the first theorists of the postmodern, Ihab Hassan, summed up the basic tenets of the postmodern as it evolved from fiction and literary theory into the fields of art, music, philosophy, anthropology and psychoanalysis (see the table overleaf).

Hassan's list suggests that, far from opposing modernism, postmodernism contains many of the fundamental aesthetic principles of modernism. Virtually all the characteristics of the postmodern enumerated by Hassan existed within modernism, from Joyce's antinarrative in *Ulysses* to the role of chance, play and anarchy in Dadaism and Surrealism and the music of Erik Satie. In his ballet *Parade* (1921), Satie included a typewriter and revolver as part of the orchestra, while other composers consciously sought to incorporate the sounds and

Modernism	Postmodernism
Form (closed)	Antiform (closed)
Purpose	Play
Design	Chance
Hierarchy	Anarchy
Art object/Finished work	Process/Performance/Happening
Distance	Participation
Centring	Dispersal
Paradigm	Syntagm
Depth	Surface
Interpretation/Reading	Against interpretation/Misreading
Signified	Signifier
Narrative	Antinarrative
Determinacy	Indeterminacy
Transcendence	Immanence

(Adapted from Hassan, 1993, p. 152)

fleeting experiences of the new urban civilisation, the steam engine in Honegger's *Pacific 231*, the football match in Martinu's *Half-Time*. Much of this modern music is close to the Dadaist aesthetic, art as happening and process, as anarchy opposing tradition, internally pre-figuring the postmodern. Such examples suggest the difficulties of distinguishing modernism from postmodernism, and provide support for Lyotard's argument that as modernism becomes worn out and exhausted aesthetically, postmodernism emerges as a new form of modernism. In contrast, Bakhtin's cultural sociology suggests that an explanation of the specifics of modernism and postmodernism must entail close exploration of the complex linkages between the internal elements and structures and the broader cultural and social context. Other early critics (Clement Greenberg and Lionel Trilling, for example) attacked the postmodern as kitsch, the cultural exemplar of commercialised and populist values. Building on this literary and aesthetic analysis, Daniel Bell in his *The Cultural Contradictions of Capitalism* (1979) attempted to contextualise postmodernism socio-logically by linking it to the development of post-capitalist and post-industrial society.

For Bell, post-industrialism signifies the advance of information technology and 'theoretical knowledge' as axial principles which determine 'social innovation and the direction of social change'. Bell's main point is that these developments portend radical changes in the social and occupational structure from an economy based on the mass production of goods through labour-intensive industry, to a service economy dominated by new professional and technical strata. Post-industrial society embraces the principles of mass consumption of both goods and services, and Bell argues that the ascetic-rational principles which formed the cultural roots of modern capitalism are gradually eroded. The adverserial, subversive nature of modernism effectively undermines the ascetic-rational principles of Protestant culture: modernist culture is the triumph of pleasure, antinomianism and anti-institutionalism, a 'rage' against order, bourgeois values and society. Modernist culture erodes the values of work, sobriety, frugality and sexual restraint; and as the culmination of modernism, postmodernist culture celebrates a hedonistic world of mass consumption, fashion, photography, advertising and travel, a culture imbricated in play, fun, display and unrestrained pleasure (Bell, 1979, pp. 46–7, 71).

The moral basis of modern capitalism, according to Bell, is thus in danger of collapse. With the exhaustion of modernism, the postmodern inevitably leads to a culture that is prodigal, promiscuous, anti-rational and anti-intellectual, in which the positive vestiges of modernism (its 'brilliant explorations of style and its dazzling experiments of form' and a literature built around the heightening of experience and concern with spiritual salvation) are annulled. Aesthetic experience is reduced to impulse, pleasure and the instinctual (ibid., pp. 115–18).

While modernism maintains the principle of aesthetic autonomy within the art work itself, the postmodern creates a new bond between art and life. Bell suggests that as the traditional class structure 'dissolves', with individuals increasingly seeking identity through 'cultural tastes and life styles' rather than through work and occupational status, a culture emerges dominated by hedonism and an art emptied of that tension which acts as the source of creativity and engagement with the past. Bell's point is that the 'eclipse of distance', the inability of the spectator or reader to stand back and engage in dialogue with the art work, implies a profound loss of a sense of the past, of the continuity of the past with the present. Postmodern culture presents no ordering principles of experience and judgement, only immediacy, impact, sensation and simultaneity.

For Bell, then, the problem of modernity is fundamentally the problem of belief, with postmodernism leading to a splitting up and disintegration of the whole (ibid., p. 27). His analysis is curiously reminiscent of certain Marxist theories which equally lament the loss of the sense of wholeness under capitalism and the need for unifying social values. But this is not the role of modernist culture. Openness, difference, ambiguity, decentred interaction are the stuff of modernist culture, promoting a healthy scepticism towards authority, power and hierarchy. Bell, in effect, deradicalises Weber's thesis on the partial autonomy of spheres, arguing for an overarching world view that will generate the values necessary for a unified and common culture.

In effect, Bell wants to have his cake and eat it. The autonomisation of culture and the rise of modernism can be connected only very loosely with economic motivation and ascetic social practices and values. The development of modernism was never simply the result of an anti-bourgeois and anti-capitalist ideology, as Bell implies, but a complex response to the culture of modernity and its capitalist basis in market principles. The increasing commodification and commercialisation of art within market-oriented capitalism threatens the autonomy of art itself. Through its imagery, artistic devices and poetic language, modernism projects an alternative reality, a utopian and subversive aesthetic standing apart from the 'inauthentic' and 'degraded' forms of commercialised mass culture. This is the critical distinction between postmodernism and modernism, for while both may share similar internal elements and forms, it is the postmodern which seeks a rapprochement with contemporary capitalism, eroding the boundaries between culture and society. Thus, while Bell's analysis focusses on the disintegration of culture and the necessity for a new moral centre, the postmodern rejects such totalising conceptions and celebrates the ultimate collapse of differentiating principles. The postmodern can thus be analysed as the annihilation of 'the great divide' between high and popular culture (Huyssen, 1986).

Postmodernism, Mass Culture and the Logic of Capitalism

Within the postmodern, image replaces narrative: postmodern architecture mixes images and styles while rejecting the metanarrative of modernist architecture (the rational, scientific, functional ordering of space); postmodern film emphasises spectacle and images which recycle the cinematic past, eroding a sense of time and space and abolishing realist narrative. While Bell's sociological account sees nothing positive in these developments, Frederick Jameson's analysis of the postmodern is celebratory and affirmative. Like Bell, Jameson seeks to contextualise the postmodern by linking its development with specific features of modern, or 'late', capitalism and, therefore, by establishing continuity and not a rupture from modernity and modernism.

Employing a traditional Marxist framework, Jameson argues that capitalism develops through three distinct stages, market capitalism, monopoly capitalism and multinational capitalism. Each stage is characterised by a specific 'cultural dominant' – aesthetic realism, modernism and postmodernism. On the basis of Ernest Mandel's theory of three capitalist epochs, Jameson describes the post-1945 period as 'late capitalism', which constitutes 'the purest form of capital yet to have emerged, a prodigious expansion of capital into hitherto uncommodified areas' (Jameson, 1991, pp. 35–6). A new type of social life and economic order has emerged as a 'purer and more homogeneous expression of classical capitalism' in which postmodernism is effectively a mode of production and not simply a cultural category (ibid., p. 406). Postmodern cultural production thus penetrates to all areas of late capitalist society, incorporating and institutionalising modernism itself, transforming the 'formerly oppositional' movement into a 'set of dead classics' no longer able to shock and scandalise but 'received with the greatest complacency... at one with the official or public culture of Western society' (ibid., p. 4). And as a mode of production, not style, postmodernism is hegemonic, in contrast to the cultural dominants of aesthetic realism and modernism which coexisted with other cultural tendencies and movements.

Clearly opposed to Weber's separation of spheres, Jameson argues that the relative autonomy of culture belongs to the early stages of capitalism, for with the expansion of global, multinational capital, culture expands 'prodigiously' through all social realms 'to the point at which everything in our social life – from economic value and state power' is cultural 'in some original and yet untheorised sense' (ibid., p. 48). But if everything has become cultural, how is it possible to make any useful analytical distinctions between different forms of practices, values, meaning, institutions and artefacts? What is the distinction between culture and non-culture? Within postmodern society everything has become commodified, rendering such distinctions irrelevant. Thus postmodern art celebrates the commodification of culture: Andy Warhol's Coca-Cola bottles and Campbell soup tins synthesise the aesthetic image with commodity fetishism without the critical cutting edge of modernist art. Warhol's images, like all commodities, have a depthless quality which for Jameson constitutes their strength as exemplars of postmodern culture.

In his analysis of postmodernism, Jameson identifies four crucial elements which differentiate it from modernism:

1. Postmodernism constitutes a cultural force field in which coexisting and 'diverse elements' are brought together in a structural unity. A cultural dominant functions hegemonically to integrate heterogeneous forces into a cultural whole.

2. Postmodernism abolishes aesthetic distance: a modernist painting such as Munch's *The Scream*, for example, conveys an authentic, uncommodified experience of alienation, solitude and fragmentation inspiring respect and awe in the viewer.

3. Postmodernism heralds a weakening of historicity, an immersion in the present to the exclusion of any real sense of historical time. Jameson cites E. L. Doctorow's *Ragtime* as an historical novel set in turn-of-the-century America, in which the historical past is not 'represented', only 'our' ideas and stereotypes of the past. In sharp contrast, Kafka's *The Trial* juxtaposes the culture of modernity – especially urbanism and alienation – with the archaic, baroque elements of an enigmatic court, a modernising economy coexisting with residual political and legal culture. Postmodernist culture thus abolishes the archaic to leave no trace, no sense of the past and no memory. Jameson suggests that in Scott's historical novels the cultural dominant of aesthetic realism allowed the archaic to play a critical role through dramatising the contrast between a new mode of production and the old, residual feudal social relations (ibid., p. 405).

4. The dominant normative element within postmodern culture is pastiche, which mimics and randomly 'cannibalises' the styles of the past. Repetition and eclecticism further work to efface the 'frontier between high culture and so-called mass or commercial culture' with the various postmodernisms drawn irresistibly to a 'landscape of schlock and kitsch, of TV series and *Reader's Digest* culture, of advertising and motels, of the late-show and the grade-B Hollywood film ... the popular biography, the murder mystery and the science fiction or fantasy novel materials they no longer simply

'quote', as a Joyce or a Mahler might have done, but incorporate into their very substance' (ibid., pp. 2–3). Postmodernism is, moreover, a global phenomenon, its dynamism flowing from the multinational economy and the new forms of electronic media.

Jameson's thesis, while overlapping with some other versions of postmodernism, offers some striking differences. Although theorised within the literary–aesthetic and political paradigm which has played such a key role in the analysis of both modernity and postmodernity, Jameson analyses postmodernism at the macro not the micro level, employing Marxist concepts such as mode of production and totality and proposing what seems close to a meta-narrative. To theorise postmodernism as a mode of production and cultural dominant suggests not the irreducibility and heterogeneity of postmodern culture but rather an integrating and unifying process in which 'difference' is assimilated to an underlying structure.

Unlike Weber's differentiation of cultural spheres, postmodernism is de-differentiation, a process in which culture 'impacts' back into social, economic and political life 'in ways that make any independent . . . extra cultural form of it problematical' (ibid., p. 277). But Jameson claims that other, non-postmodern tendencies coexist within the structure of the force field, although his notion of cultural dominant is conceived in this context as hegemonic (unlike aesthetic realism and modernism). This formulation is clearly indebted to Williams's distinction between emergent, residual and dominant culture which I discussed and criticised in Chapter 5. Like Williams, Jameson fails to explain how other forces within the field develop a partial autonomy from the dominant culture. Moreover, there is no analysis of the complex relation between different forms of cultural production within the force field. Indeed, there is little sense in Jameson's model of any complex play of forces at work within the field, rather that such forces become assimilated and integrated through a totalising process which connects the different postmodern forms, from architecture (closely bound up with economics) to film and painting, to the mode of production. As I suggested in discussing Bourdieu's theory of field, a totalising model of cultural production will emphasise integration rather than dispersion and struggle. A force field is structured in difference, opposition and struggle; the specific forces at work produce changes in the structure of the field itself and the cultural artefacts produced. But Jameson's model offers no principles of change at work with the force field, no analysis of the specific social groups involved in the different forms of cultural production and reproduction, the positions they occupy and the relations between them.

In effect, Jameson reduces the highly complex, differentiated and hierarchical structure of modern capitalist society, the institutions and the practices and struggles of agents within cultural production, to a deterministic historical narrative which blindly unfolds behind the backs of agents. The concept of narrative is a key element in Jameson's theory, because as a totalising process narrative enables individuals to make sense of their lives and project the possibility of recovering the unity of social life which was lost with the capitalist division of labour (Jameson, 1981, p. 226). Such Hegelian, Frankfurt School, essentialist ideas seem to run counter both to the concept of the postmodern itself and to Jameson's own analysis of it as a culture emptied of historical meaning, structured in the norms of immediacy and celebratory of commodity fetishism.

A further problem lies in the periodisation schema. Mandel's concept of late capitalism is located in the immediate post-1945 period, but Jameson's postmodernism emerges during the 1960s. Moreover, capitalist production passed through a number of distinctive phases from the 1940s to the 1980s, from the centralised government interventionism linked with Keynesian economics to the free market ideology of Reagan and Thatcher. And David Harvey has pointed to the post-Fordist phase of the 1970s involving smaller and flexible economic units than those associated with 'organised capitalism' (Harvey, 1989, ch 10). In Jameson's analysis the specifics of capitalist economic production are vaguely and abstractly articulated, with postmodern culture linked in a broad and direct mode with the productive process. In late capitalism, culture has become the central productive force, no longer separate from the economic: the concepts of the cultural and the economic 'thereby collapse back into one another and say the same thing, in an eclipse of the distinction between base and superstructure [so that] the base, in the third stage of capitalism, generates its superstructures with a new kind of dynamic' (ibid., p. xxi). But there is little compelling empirical evidence to support Jameson's model of postmodern culture. Modern capitalism remains hierarchically structured, its institutions generating inequalities of income, property and culture. And these institutions vary in their degree of autonomy. Mass culture, or postmodernist culture, may enjoy little autonomy, but it does not follow that all culture – the different levels, institutions and collective agents – is tarred with the same conflationist and deterministic brush.

While Jameson's speculative attempts to contextualise postmodernism culture is indebted to Marxist economic theory, his analysis of the forms themselves has been influenced by the work of Jean Baudrillard, one of the gurus of the postmodern, a lapsed Marxist and professional academic sociologist. In his articles 'The Order of Simulacra' (1976) and 'The Precession of Simulacra' (1981), Baudrillard advanced a theory of the postmodern as a 'hyperreal' culture dominated by images and simulacra or copies without originals. History no longer refers to anything real, to meaning, to truth. Abandoning Marx's distinction between use and exchange value, Baudrillard argues that postmodern culture is dominated by 'sign value', by commodities conferring status and power. In today's 'semiurgic society', postmodernism constitutes a culture in which the 'real' has been assimilated to the image. Signs no longer refer to an external, objective reality; they have become reality. Images bear no relation with reality: the hyperreal is constantly reproduced through the electronic media, so that, as he notes in 'The Ecstasy of Communication' (1983a), advertising and television invade all the 'most intimate processes of our social life'.

Baudrillard's postmodernism is thus a culture of passivity: the hyperreal becomes the real, so that Disneyland is the 'real' America:

> Disneyland is there to conceal the fact that it is the 'real' country, all of 'real' America, which is Disneyland ... Disneyland is presented as imaginary in order to make us believe that the rest is real, when in fact all of Los Angeles and the America surrounding it are no longer real, but of the order of the hyperreal and of simulation. (Baudrillard, 1983b)

All boundaries have been abolished, reality has 'imploded' and the traditional sociological notion of the social has disappeared. Baudrillard presents a social landscape emptied of all structural processes, institutions and agents: society consists of a vast, phantasmagoric superstructure of signs and images to which the individual has neither an objective nor alienated relationship. Postmodern culture abhors active agents for the individual is no longer an actor but rather 'a terminal of multiple networks' including television, computers, telephones, micro-satellites. Modern mass culture, with its 'useless hyperinformation', fabricates non-communication in that no active exchange occurs between the production of images and their reception, the mass media forcing silence on the masses and plunging them into a 'state of stupor' (Baudrillard, 1983a).

As with Jameson, Baudrillard fails to make any connections between the processes of consumption and the productive process. All his examples of the postmodern exist within determinate social structures and involve highly complex chains of authority. Who makes decisions in the media, who constructs the images and who decides how they are to be marketed? The media consist of highly organised and hierarchical organisations in which the investment of capital plays a key role. Who invests, who takes decisions and who controls the media? Although Baudrillard is right to emphasise the development of a culture dominated by mass media, his approach is designed to simplify the mechanics of communication and the problems of power and authority.

Concluding Remarks: The Problem of Modernity, History and Postmodernism

If modernity was differentiation (Weber's spheres) and autonomisation, then postmodernity is de-differentiation (Baudrillard's 'implosion'). In Jameson's analysis the logic of modern capitalism is towards a new culture, populist and democratic, in which the elision of boundaries between high–popular–mass culture and between the economic, political and cultural signifies a loss of the historical sense. Individuals now live in the instantaneous present, a present emptied of all living, meaningful links with the past. But modernity itself has frequently been theorised in broadly similar terms, as a culture which breaks decisively from the past, erasing history in favour of the 'newness' of the present. Moreover, by breaking from tradition and history, modernity generated what Bell has called the problem of belief, the lack of a unifying set of values which hold society together. I have argued, however, that modernity does not necessarily entail these gloomy and pessimistic conclusions. Marx, for example, identifies the structural basis of modernity in the dynamic and expanding nature of capitalist production, and although his work is problematic in relation to agency and historical narrative, it does provide a historical context for the energy, restless activity and purposiveness of modernity as experience (Baudelaire). Equally, Bakhtin's theory of culture as internally differentiated and decentred, a pluralism involving struggles between many voices within contexts that are profoundly historical, suggests a concept of modernity open and unfinalised. The dialogic principle opposes all sense of closed, integrated cultures and societies built around a dominant belief system. Modernity is thus the celebration of healthy relativism, scepticism towards authority and grand, finalising narratives, and acceptance of the irreducible pluralism, differences and ambiguity of social life.

Marx, however, while analysing the structural basis of modernity, yokes it to the grand narrative of emancipation of the proletariat and the necessary development of capitalism towards highly integrated socialist systems. There is, then, a strong finalising discourse running through Marx's analysis of modernity contradicting his emphasis on action, culture and (as I noted in Chapter 1) collective agents. But, in general, Marx's work is ambiguous in these areas, the emphasis on autonomy, for example, being assimilated to the overarching historical narrative.

Bakhtin's work is important also for its analysis of boundaries. To argue that culture exists on boundaries is not to collapse all differentiated structures, to abandon all notions of an objective historical context, to grasp the hierarchical structures of culture itself. This is the cul-de-sac into which the theories of postmodern culture are plunged (Jameson, Baudrillard and Foucault), failing to engage sociologically and historically with new forms of cultural production emerging out of new fields and social struggles.

Conclusion

In this book I have argued that the modern concept of culture arose simultaneously with the idea of modernity, and that the development of industrial capitalism, with its technological and urban-based infrastructure, laid the basis for the autonomisation of culture into distinctive spheres or fields, institutions and practices each structured in terms of specific internal logics and properties. In the work of Weber, Durkheim, Parsons, Bakhtin and Bourdieu, culture comes to occupy a privileged position, its structure and forms linked to specific social and historical contexts yet partly autonomous of social structure, institutions and social interaction. Locating culture contextually while preserving the principle of autonomy constitutes one of the most difficult problems in the sociology of culture. Although many cultural theorists acknowledge the autonomy principle, there is a strong tendency to collapse the concept of culture into the concept of society: Durkheim, Parsons and the Frankfurt School, for example, theorise culture partly in terms of its role in securing social integration, while simultaneously arguing that culture always involves immanent, transcendent universal values. Both Durkheim and Parsons acknowledge that the morally binding elements of culture flow from a universal core of values producing normative integration. Similiarly, Gramsci's notion of hegemony implies a universal, ethical, cultural core capable of commanding the loyalty of both subordinate and dominant classes, while for the Frankfurt School culture is both commodified into culture industry and yet in essence affirming a critical and utopian potential.

174

Modernity, too, must be grounded sociologically. Too often the concept of modernity has been loosely defined in terms of a complex of ideas (such as the philosophy of the Enlightenment) to the exclusion of its specific historical infrastructure. Much of the literature on modernity is speculative, philosophical, impressionistic and literary, inadequately contextualising the complex processes leading to the genesis of different modernities and offering few concepts to link the various forms of modernity with social and historical forms and structures. Thus the aesthetic definition of modernity, with its emphasis on subjective experience, on the fleeting and emphemeral forms of social life, can easily degenerate into intellectual journalism and vacuous, decontextualised speculation.

There is, too, the problem of periodisation: if modernity is described in terms of Weber's differentiation thesis then it raises questions concerning broadly similar processes in pre-capitalist societies such as Renaissance Italy, in which culture, economy and politics were closely bound together yet allowed space for the development of aesthetic autonomy. Moreover, I have suggested that the differentiation thesis forms the backbone of a sociology of modernity, without attributing this process mechanically to modern rationalised capitalism, because embryonic spheres or fields coexisted with nascent capitalism and industrialism. The key to understanding modernity lies in the different forms of civil society generated by capitalist development and the cultural institutions linked with it. During the late eighteenth century, cultural production and producers increasingly became independent of pre-capitalist modes of centralised political authority and patronage: while Haydn remained a court composer almost to the end of his life, Mozart broke free of ecclesiastical and monarchical patronage to become the first modern composer, writing for subscription concerts and a distinctive middle-class public which had built an infrastructure of civil society in the Vienna of the 1780s. The careers of Mozart, Beethoven and Rossini embody the fundamental principle of modernity: the erosion of the power of the centre in modern culture with the development of a market for cultural artefacts, the professionalisation of the cultural producers and the genesis of institutions to regulate and legitimate the pluralism of cultural production as a whole. This constitutes the sociological core of the decentring of the social world.

Moreover, modernity, like culture, involves action, human agents in processes of making. It is misleading to identify the genesis of modernity as an inevitable process of rationality leading to a decentred world, because the institutions and values which make this possible are the products of collective action taking place within particular socio-cultural contexts. Action must be linked with institutions and broader social forces. Habermas has noted that the modernity project does not work behind the backs of agents, but involves a fluid and open dialogue between specialists and the public and ultimately within the ideal speech community. Modernity is made within the life-world, and while money, power and system imperatives may threaten the potential autonomy of the cultural world, emancipation remains a genuine possibility. I am suggesting that Habermas's theory of modernity (which in many ways is at odds with his general social theory) implicitly suggests a role for responsible human agents who possess the necessary reflexive qualities to produce change.

In contrast to Habermas, Giddens explicitly links modernity with reflexivity. For Giddens, the concept of 'high modernity' emphasises the open and plural nature of modern society, with its institutions enabling individuals to make many choices and a 'diversity of autonomies'. The modern self is reflexively made; high modernity assumes an increasing purposiveness to human activity with increasing control over the conditions of social reproduction. One of Giddens's main points is the extent to which sociological knowledge itself enters and transforms social life with the emergence of 'expert systems' involving doctors, counsellors, therapists and dieticians, whose knowledge becomes part of everyday life in helping to shape the individual's sense of identity. High modernity is thus characterised by the self as a reflexive project, with action constantly monitored by institutions. The culture of high modernity is hence partly autonomous, with knowledge and expert systems enhancing the reflexive nature of self and its relation with society (Giddens, 1991).

While Giddens's concept of high modernity is clearly grounded in a specific sociological context, it breaks decisively from the argument presented in this book. Giddens rejects the salience of the differentiation thesis, arguing that it is no longer relevant in the age of global media and transnational corporations. The processes of globalisation have transformed the nature of social relations effectively, removing them from local contexts and relocating them across infinite spans of time and space. Place itself becomes 'phantasmagoric' as distant events, institutions and decision-making intrude into everyday life and consciousness.

Giddens's work brings us to the heart of the problem of modernity. Although he has stressed both its inherent reflexivity and its basis in new forms of social organisation (thus distinguishing high modernity from postmodernism, which mainly refers to aesthetic reflections on modernity and artistic styles and movements), Giddens overstates the erosion of local institutions and cultures, and remains vague on the actual mechanisms regulating the transmission and reception both of sociological and expert knowledge. There is a danger that Giddens is reducing modernity to the single dimension of reflexivity and failing to engage with the problem of contradictions. Within the concept of modernity a tension is generated between the undoubted potential for the development of human freedom and autonomy through the expansion of culture, civil society and its institutions, and the controls exercised over freedom and autonomy by the modern centralised state (the darker side of modernity) as it seeks to assimilate all differences, such as language and ethnic culture, to an underlying centre. As the culture industry concept suggests, the centralising trends implicit within modernity can silence alternative voices, values and arguments, imposing a monologic unity over the whole society. Hence the crucial importance of culture for understanding modernity: for culture unlocks the dialogic potential within it, affirming difference and pluralism, open and unfinalised discourses and structures.

Finally, we come to the problems of a sociology of culture.

1. Within the field of cultural sociology a wide range of meanings and definitions proliferate – Adorno's affirmative and utopian essence, Geertz's rigorously contextualised notion of meaning, Durkheim's collective symbols, rituals and representations, and Williams's whole way of life. There is, too, Gramsci's and Bakhtin's analysis of the inherent democracy and ambivalence of popular culture, its dialogic, critical and subversive potential, its living links with everyday life and the ways culture is made and remade through social struggles. A cultural sociology must provide a critique of these differing concepts and tease out the complex and subtle relations between different forms of cultural production, cultural institutions and cultural practices. If modernity is structured in distinctive historical contexts and reflexivity, then culture is equally reflexive

and context-bound. In this book I have argued against those theorists, from Durkheim and Parsons to the Frankfurt School, who reduce culture to a single dimension – cultural institutions and symbolic forms underpinning social order – while simultaneously searching for universal, transcendent values. However, a distinction must be made between the concept of a common culture built around the fixed nature of everyday life and culture industry with its critical rejection of a reifed and commodified everyday world which subverts the 'otherness' of culture.

2. It is essential to go beyond functionalist sociologies of culture, to theorise and rethink the relation of the cultural and symbolic to the social by incorporating a sociological notion of active agent. Parsons's common culture, while rejecting the crude reduction of culture to everyday modes of social interaction and social context, does not address the problem of reflexivity, attempting rather to synthesise transcendent elements (derived from Kantian philosophical categories) with functionalist holism and teleology. To theorise culture in terms of universal values is sociologically unacceptable, if universality is defined in terms of fixed and unchanging, timeless values. If there is a universal and transcendent core to culture then it has been made through the forging and shaping of new institutions and values. The universal may be conceived sociologically as a deposit from within this process, embodied in cultural forms and artefacts and open to revision and change (religious symbols, the idea of democracy and justice, aesthetic genres never finalised and complete within themselves).

3. All variations on the myth of cultural integration, with its central tenet of societies cohering around a centre of commonly held values, must be abandoned. Culture is always imbricated in social and ideological struggles, and has no neutral or disinterested basis. Gramsci's hegemony, Bakhtin's dialogism and Bourdieu's field theory define culture as resistence and opposition, involving active, reflexive agents whose collective actions shape the social and cultural world in *difference*.

4. The question of partial autonomy requires the development of adequate conceptual tools to facilitate empirical–historical analysis of the structural basis of autonomisation. Too often, cultural theorists advance concepts which assimilate culture to social practices

and vague notions of praxis. The principle of autonomy does not arise out of ideas, but is generated out of specific social and economic forces, or infrastructure, in definite historical contexts. The process of the autonomisation of culture will vary in tempo, depth and extent from one society to another (influenced by such elements as economics and politics, intellectual and cultural traditions, market forces, etc.) and within the same society (for example, the autonomisation of the subfield of the novel developed in England during the nineteenth century but not that of opera, while in Germany during the same period the process was largely the opposite). There is uneven and combined development within the autonomisation process.

5. To theorise culture in terms of partial autonomy raises the question of voluntarism and reflexivity. While culture is analytically distinct from social practices, such practices necessarily enter as constituting elements in the making of culture. Culture is critical and reflexive, its making linked with understanding, knowledge and historicity: the partial autonomy of culture develops both immanently (aesthetic forms shaping the material *and* content of a work for example) and structurally. Culture in its making becomes a dialogue between the present and the past, a realm of memory which establishes historical continuity between the nowness and meaning of the present with living elements from the past, a dialogue involving many different voices seeking to establish an identity and presence within the present, responsive and alive to others. The constituting role of dialogue in culture cannot be exaggerated: the culture of modernity is decentred and built around differences at all levels of society, differences which abhor all modes of centralisation. Dialogue points to the pluralism of culture, its hybrid nature. The many voices of the cultures of modernity find their unity through dialogical interaction forging their independence and uniqueness.

6. The hybrid nature of culture suggests a postmodern standpoint. I have argued against the prognoses and concepts of postmodern theory. Culture is analysed contextually, and cultural sociology should avoid the short circuit effect by bringing to light the complex play of forces, embracing both structure and action, at work within particular contexts. Culture is not simply an expression of

the ideology, or world view, of a social class but the result of a highly fluid, socio-historical field of forces. Concepts of field elaborated within postmodern theory (notably by Jameson) contextualise inadequately, failing both to explicate the precise forces at work, the links between the micro and macro levels, and to ground the actions of social agents within a structured context, that is, a hierarchially ordered one. It is essential to avoid the false dualisms of agency and structure, micro and macro, incorporating the interaction order within the larger force field, grasping the ways in which interaction and objective 'positionality' reinforce each other in analysis. As I have noted, the instrumental nature of action in Bourdieu's cultural theory is related to his failure to develop a theory of interaction within a structural context, to address the issue of the making of culture through dialogue and communication by those participants who commit themselves through a reflexive consciousness of culture and its enduring value for human society.

Bibliography

Adorno, T. W. (1973) 'Letters to Walter Benjamin', *New Left Review*, no. 81.
—— (1976), *Introduction to the Sociology of Music* (New York: Seabury Press).
—— (1981) *In Search of Wagner* (London: Verso).
—— (1984) *Aesthetic Theory* (London: Routledge & Kegan Paul).
—— (1989) 'Society' in *Critical Theory and Society: A Reader* (London: Routledge & Kegan Paul).
—— (1991) *The Culture Industry:Selected Essays on Mass Culture* (London: Routledge & Kegan Paul).
Adorno, T. W. and Horkheimer, M. (1973) *Dialectic of Enlightenment* (London: New Left Books).
Alexander, J. C. and Seidman, S. (eds.) (1990) *Culture and Society: Contemporary Debates* (Cambridge University Press).
Antal, F. (1986) *Florentine Painting and its Social Background* (London: Harvard University Press).
Archer, M. (1989) *Culture and Agency* (Cambridge University Press).
Bakhtin, M. M. (1968) *Rabelais and his World* (London: MIT Press).
—— (1981) *The Dialogic Imagination* (London, University of Texas Press).
—— (1984) *Problems of Dostoevsky's Poetics* (Manchester University Press).
—— (1986) *Speech Genres and Other Late Essays* (London: University of Texas Press).
—— (1990) *Art and Answerability* (London: University of Texas Press).
Bakhtin, M. M. and Volosinov, V. N. (1973) *Marxism and the Philosophy of Language* (London: Harvard University Press).
Baudelaire, C. (1972) *Selected Writings* (London: Penguin).
Baudrillard, J. (1983a) 'The Ecstasy of Communication', in H. Foster (ed.) *Postmodern Culture* (London: Pluto Press).
Baudrillard, J. (1983b) *Simulations* (New York: Semiotext).
Baxandall, M. (1988), *Painting and Experience in Fifteenth Century Italy*, 2nd edn (Oxford University Press).

182   *Bibliography*

Bell, D. (1979) *Cultural Contradictions of Capitalism* (London: Heinemann)
Benjamin, W. (1983) *Charles Baudelaire: A Lyric Poet in the Era of High Capitalism* (London: Verso).
Berman, M. (1983) *All That Is Solid Melts Into Air* (London: Verso).
Bloch, E. (1987) *The Spirit of Utopia* (New York: Seabury Press).
Bourdieu, P. (1971) 'Intellectual Field and Creative Project', in Michael F. D. Young (ed.) *Knowledge and Control: New Directions for the Sociology of Education* (London: Collier–Macmillan).
—— (1984) *Distinction: A Social Critique of the Judgement of Taste* (London: Routledge & Kegan Paul).
—— (1990a) *The Logic of Practice* (Oxford: Polity Press).
—— (1990b) *Photography: A Middle-Brow Art* (Oxford: Polity Press).
—— (1993a) *Sociology in Question* (London: Sage).
—— (1993b) *The Field of Cultural Production* (Oxford: Polity Press).
—— (1996) *The Love of Art* (Oxford: Polity Press).
Bourdieu, P. and Wacquant, L. J. D. (1992) *An Invitation to Reflexive Sociology* (Oxford: Polity Press).
Bourricard, F. (1981) *The Sociology of Talcott Parsons* (London: University of Chicago Press).
Calhoun, C. (1995) *Bourdieu: Critical Perspectives* (Oxford, Polity Press).
Calinescu, M. (1997) *Faces of Modernity* (London: Indiana University Press).
Clark, K. and Holquist, M. (1984) *Mikhail Bakhtin* (London: Harvard University Press).
Clark, T. J. (1973) *Image of the People: Gustave Courbet and the 1848 Revolution.* (London: Thames & Hudson)
Dahlmann, D. (1987) Max Weber's Relation to Anarchism and Anarchists: the Case of Ernst Toller', in Mommsen, W. J. and Osterhammwl, J. (eds), *Max Weber and His Contemporaries* (London: Unwin Hyman).
Durkheim, E. (1957) *The Elementary Forms of the Religious Life* (London: Allen & Unwin).
—— (1982) The Rules of Sociological Method and Selected Texts on Sociology and Its Method (London: Macmillan).
Eichenbaum, B. (1978) 'Literary Environment', in L. Matejka and K. Pomorska (eds), *Readings from Russian Poetics* (Cambridge, Mass: MIT Press).
Erlich, V. (1981) *Russian Formalism* (New Haven, Conn.: Yale University Press).
Fiedler, L. (1992) 'Cross the Border – Close the Gap', in P. Waugh (ed.), *Postmodernism: A Reader* (London, Edward Arnold).
Foucault, M. (1986) *The Foucault Reader* (London: Penguin).
—— (1988) *Politics, Philosophy, Culture* (London: Routledge & Kegan Paul).
Frisby, D. (1985) *Fragments of Modernity* (Cambridge: Blackwell).
Garfinkel, H. (1967) *Studies in Ethnomethodology* (Englewood Cliffs, NJ: Prentice-Hall).
Geertz, C. (1973) *The Interpretation of Cultures; Selected Essays* (New York: Basic Books).

Giddens, A. (1987) *Social Theory and Modern Sociology* (Oxford: Polity Press).
Giddens, A. (1991) *The Consequences of Modernity* (Oxford: Polity Press).
Goffman, E. (1961) *Asylums* (New York: Anchor Books).
——(1972) *Interaction Ritual* (London: Penguin Books).
——(1981) *Forms of Talk* (Oxford: Blackwell).
——(1983) 'The Interaction Order', in *American Sociological Review*, 48.
Goldmann, (1964) *The Hidden God* (London: Routledge).
Gramsci, A. (1972) *Selections from the Prison Notebooks* (London: Lawrence & Wishart)
——(1977) *Selections from Political Writings, 1910–1920* (London: Lawrence & Wishart).
——(1978) *Selections from Political Writings, 1921–1926* (London, Lawrence & Wishart).
——(1985) *Selections from Cultural Writings* (London, Lawrence & Wishart).
Griswold, W. (1986) *Renaissance Revivals: City Comedy and Revenge Tragedy in the London Theatre 1576–1980* (University of Chicago Press).
Habermas, J. (1979) *Communication and the Evolution of Society* (London: Heinemann).
——(1985) 'Modernity: An Incomplete Project', in H. Foster (ed.), *Postmodern Culture* (London: Pluto Press).
——(1987) *The Philosophical Discourse of Modernity* (Oxford: Polity Press).
Hall, S. (1996) 'For Allon White: Metaphors of Transformation', in D. Morley and K-H. Chen (eds), *Stuart Hall: Critical Dialogues* (London: Routledge & Kegan Paul)
Harvey, D. (1989) *The Condition of Postmodernity* (Oxford: Blackwell).
Hassan, I. (1993) 'Towards a concept of postmodern', in T. Docherty (ed.), *Postmodernism A Reader* (London: Harvester).
Hauser, A. (1963) *The Philosophy of Art History* (New York: Meridian Books).
Hoggart, R. (1957) *The Uses of Literacy* (London: Penguin Books).
Holquist, M. (1990) *Dialogism* (London: Routledge & Kegan Paul).
Horkheimer, M. (1972) *Critical Theory* (New York: Seabury Press).
Howe, I. (1992) 'Mass Society and Postmodern Fiction', in P. Waugh (ed.) *Postmodernism: A Reader*. (London, Edward Arnold).
Huyssen, A. (1986) *After the Great Divide: Modernism, Mass Culture, Postmodernism* (London: Macmillan).
Jameson, F. (1981) *The Political Unconscious* (London. Methuen).
——(1991) *Postmodernism* (London: Verso).
Jay, M. (1984) *Adorno* (London: Fontana).
——(1993) *Force Fields: Between Intellectual History and Cultural Critique* (London: Routledge & Kegan Paul)
Keating, P. J. (1989) *The Haunted House* (London: Hodder)
Kumar, K. (1995) *From Post-Industrial to Post-Modern society* (Oxford: Blackwell).
Le Roy Ladurie, E. (1981) *Carnival in Romans* (tr. M. Feeney) (Harmondsworth: Penguin)
Lukács, G. (1964) *Studies in European Realism* (New York: Grossett & Dunlap).

Lyotard, J.-F. (1989) *The Lyotard Reader*, ed. A. Benjamin (Oxford: Blackwell).
Mannheim, K. (1953) *Essays in Sociology and Social Psychology* (London: Routledge & Kegan Paul).
—— (1982) *Structures of Thinking* (London: Routledge & Kegan Paul)
Marcuse, H. (1968) *Negations* (London: Allen Lane).
Marinetti, F. T. (1996) 'The Founding and Manifesto of Futurism', in L. Cahoone (ed.), *From Modernism to Postmodernism: An Anthology* (Oxford: Blackwell).
Marx, K. (1958) Capital, vol. i (London: Lawrence & Wishart).
—— (1971) *A Contribution to the Critique of Political Economy* (London: Lawrence & Wishart).
—— (1973) *Grundrisse* (London: Penguin)
Marx, K. and Engels, F. (1958) *Selected Works* vol. i (London: Lawrence & Wishart).
—— (1962) *Selected Works*, vol. ii (London: Lawrence & Wishart).
—— (1965) *The German Ideology* (London: Lawrence & Wishart).
—— (1976) *On Literature and Art* (London: Lawrence & Wishart).
Medvedev, P. and Bakhtin, M. (1978) *The Formal Method in Literary Scholarship* (London: Johns Hopkins University Press).
Morley, D. (1980) *The Nationwide Audience* (London: British Film Institute).
Morson, G. S. (ed.) (1986) *Bakhtin: Essays and Dialogues on His Work* (London: University of Chicago Press).
Nietzsche, F. (1967) *The Birth of Tragedy* (New York: Vintage Books).
—— (1990) *Twilight of the Idols* (London: Penguin).
Parsons, T. (1951) *The Social System* (New York: Free Press)
—— (1955) *Family, Socialization and the Interaction Process* (New York: Free Press)
—— (1967) *Sociological Theory and Modern Society* (New York: Free Press).
—— (1989) 'A Tentative Outline of American Values', *Theory, Culture and Society*, vol. 6, no. 4.
Radway, J. (1987) *Reading the Romance* (London: Verso).
Raphael, M. (1978) *The Demands of Art* (London, Routledge & Kegan Paul)
Rose, M. A. (1991) *The Post-Modern and the Post-Industrial: A Critical Analysis* (Cambridge University Press).
Saussure, F. de (1974) *Course in General Linguistics* (London: Fontana).
Shusterman, A. (1993) 'Eliot and Adorno on the Critique of Culture', *Theory, Culture and Society*, vol. 10, no. 1.
Simmel, G. (1950) *The Sociology of Georg Simmel* (New York: Free Press).
—— (1968) *The Conflict in Modern Culture, and Other Essays* (New York: The Teachers' College Press).
—— (1990) *The Philosophy of Money,* 2nd edn (London: Routledge & Kegan Paul).
—— (1991) 'Money in Modern Culture', and 'The Berlin Trade Exhibition', in *Theory, Culture and Society* vol. 8, no. 3.
Solomon, M. (1995) *Mozart* (London: Bloomsbury).
Sombart, W. (1967) *Luxury and Capitalism* (New York: Free Press).

Stallybrass, P. and White, A. (1986) *The Politics and Poetics of Transgression* (London: Methuen).

Taine, H. (1906) *History of English Literature* (London: Chatto & Windus).

Thompson, E. P. (1981) *The Making of the English Working Class* (London: Penguin Books).

—— (1993) *Customs in Common* (London: Merlin Press).

Trotsky, L. (1957) *Literature and Revolution* (New York: Russell & Russell).

Tylor, E. B. (1958) *Primitive Culture: Researches into the Development of Mythology, Philosophy, Religion, Art, and Custom* (Gloucester, Mass.: Smith).

Tynyanov, Y. (1978) 'Literary Evolution', in L. Matejka and K. Pomorska (eds), *Readings in Russian Poetics* (Cambridge, Mass.: MIT Press).

Watt, I (1962) *The Rise of the Novel* (London: Penguin Books).

Weber, M. (1948) *From Max Weber: Essays in Sociology* (London: Routledge & Kegan Paul).

—— (1978) *Economy and Society* (New Jersey: Bedminster Press).

Whimster, S. and Lash, S. (eds) (1987) *Max Weber, Rationality and Modernity* (London: Allen & Unwin).

Wilde, O. (1955) *Plays, Prose Writings and Poems* (London: Dent).

Williams, R. (1961) *Culture and Society 1780–1950* (London: Penguin).

—— (1965) *The Long Revolution* (London: Penguin)

—— (1977) *Marxism and Literature* (London: Oxford University Press).

—— (1979) *Politics and Letters: Interviews with 'New Left Review'* (London: New Left Books)

—— (1981a) *Culture* (London: Fontana)

—— (1981b) *Problems of Materialism and Culture* (London: Verso Books).

—— (1989) *The Politics of Modernism: Against the New Conformists* (London: Verso).

Index